From a Cop's Viewpoint: Investigations 101

by

M.A. Taylor

From A Cop's Viewpoint: Investigations 101

Copyright © 2013 M.A. Taylor
Print Publication July 2013

MA.Taylor@MATaylor1010.com
HTTP://www.MATaylor1010.com

Cover Art by JCOS Worldwide
Cover Novel Graphic Designs
Formatting Services by BB eBooks

Dedication

To
Pamela Moran

Okay, I stopped bitching.

Happy Now?

Seriously, thank-you for convincing me that all I know and experienced during my career in law enforcement is better served in a book for writers. Besides I got tired of waiting for the Producers of Jeopardy to get with the program and do a Tournament of Law Enforcement.

Table of Contents

Dedication...v

Acknowledgements ix

Introduction xi

Chapter 1: Areas of Responsibilities, Rank Structure: Who's really in Charge? 1

Chapter 2: Surveillance: Electronic vs. Physical 19

Chapter 3: Undercover Operations, Narcotics Investigations, Money Laundering and Informants 37

Chapter 4: Sex Crimes and Homicide 61

Chapter 5: Interviewing vs. Interrogation: Which gets the job done..73

Chapter 6: Networking: A Cop's and Your Character's Greatest Investigative Tool..89

Chapter 7: Questions I've been asked AKA Q&A.............107

Glossary 137

About the Author...146

About *From a Cop's Viewpoint Investigations: 101* 147

Acknowledgements

Janelle Denison, a great mentor and world class prodder. Thank's for the push.

Betsy' and Ann, two of the best beta readers ever. Your input and questions helped me greatly improve this book. How long before I can send you the next one? <Huge Grin>

Any and all mistakes are my own.

Introduction

It was a long, hard day at work. I'm home. I'm tired. The kids are in bed. The dishwasher's humming and I finally have a delicious moment to put my feet up and escape into a novel. I sigh with pleasure as I visualize the heroine hunker down behind a sofa as the villain searches for her in the next room. His footsteps clomp closer and I hold my breath as she flips the safety off her revolver.

Wait!

Revolver?

Revolvers don't have safeties! I fling the book against the wall and utter a curse (I am a cop after all).

I'm willing to suspend some disbelief. Heck, I'm willing to suspend loads of it, but there are some details that drive the fantasy world off the road of believability.

Consider how many times you've read about a cop meeting a suspect alone or with only one person 'backing' them up… *Hello?* Who, while carrying a large sum of money, would go meet a bad guy all by their lonesome? Definitely not another bad guy. Trust is in short supply among criminals. In fact, the way most undercover cops are 'outted' is by their willingness to do things a normal crook wouldn't.

And let's not forget how many TV and movie crooks are released from custody and escape all punishment because they weren't read their Miranda Rights... Misrepresented details like these seriously up the Fling Factor in my world. I guess I was a bit outspoken on the issue because a good friend finally prompted me to stop bitching and help correct the inaccuracies. Thus this series of books was born.

My purpose is to show writers the basic approach cops take when tackling a crime. Not all crimes are equal and not all investigations are handled the same way. (This is investigations at its basic level. Each jurisdiction or department will have a method of operating that works best for them.) So, this book is just like the Pirates' Code, more of a guideline than set in stone.

From a Cop's Viewpoint: Investigations 101, is book one. Book two will be on Narcotic Investigations followed by Sex Crimes and then Homicide Investigations.

My goal is to create an information source that writers can pick up to understand not only how a police department differs from a sheriff department, but also where State Police, FBI, DEA, CIA and Task Forces fit into the picture.

A bit about me: I entered the California Highway Patrol (CHP) Academy less than a month after my twenty-second birthday. During my seven years with the CHP, I was a Gang Officer, School Pupil Transportation Safety Officer, Drug Recognition Expert (DRE), A member of the Special Enforcement Unit (SEU), Officer-In-Charge (OIC), Field Training Officer (FTO), Court Liaison Officer, Vehicle Identification Number Officer (VIN) and more.

After seven years, I left the CHP to become a California Department of Justice (CA-CA-DOJ), Special Agent. Although I preferred to think of myself as *Extra Special*. My first assignment was with the Bureau of Narcotic Enforcement (BNE). With BNE, my duties included locating, surveillance of and dismantling clandestine methamphetamine and PCP labs, and indoor marijuana grows. CA-DOJ had me mountain climbing in order to harvest and destroy marijuana crops at CAMP – Campaign Against Marijuana Planting. I worked undercover buying and assisted with the pseudo-sale of narcotics.

While at BNE, I was assigned to a High Intensity Drug Trafficking Area Task Force (HIDTA). This Task Force was created and overseen by the Federal Drug Enforcement Agency (DEA). I was cross designated as a Special Federal Officer, this gave me Federal Law Enforcement Authority.

My HIDTA team primarily worked major narcotic traffickers. We went after high level members of Colombian and Mexican Cartels in addition to some of the more violent Los Angeles street gangs. We did this through electronic and physical surveillance. During my tenure in narcotics, I was directly involved in investigations that facilitated the take down of multiple tons each of cocaine and marijuana as well as the seizure of millions of dollars of drug money.

After I left narcotics, I worked the Division of Gambling Control (DGC), Compliance and Enforcement Section. I was tasked with ensuring all of California's tribal gaming and card clubs adhered to Tribal Gaming Compact and/or the California Gambling Control Act. Investigation of fraud cases, prostitution, illegal lotteries and various other scams were also part of my duties.

At the California Bureau of Investigation (CBI), I worked the Sexual Predator Apprehension Team (SPAT). SPAT involved sex predator registration cases, child pornography, traveler cases, computer forensics, homicide warrant project, and DNA cold cases. I also set up a Task Force with Immigration and Customs Enforcement (ICE) for the apprehension and deportation of immigrants who had been convicted as sexual predators.

A glance through my About Me Section clearly shows my greatest knowledge base for Law

Enforcement lays within the State of California, therefore most of my examples involve California Agencies. However, having worked for and with Federal Agencies and Task Forces, I have a good understanding of the Federal System and when outside of California, I operated under Federal Task Force powers.

Chapter One

Areas of Responsibilities, Rank Structure:
Who's really in Charge?

Every Law Enforcement Officer (LEO) in every Agency in the State, whether a City Cop (Los Angeles Police Department) or a County Deputy (Los Angeles County Deputy Sheriff) is able to perform their duties anywhere in the state. Federal Agencies can go anywhere in the country and several places outside the country as well. However, it is the primary task of each Agency that distinguishes them (cops) from each other.

This Chapter is divided into two sections.

Local Agencies: This covers all Law Enforcement Agencies within a State that have their powers granted by state authority.

Federal Agencies: Those agencies that receive their powers from federal law.

In my opinion, this is where the Agency rivalries begin. Do not get me wrong, there is infighting and bickering between city, county and state agencies as well. In fact officers/agents with a state Law Enforcement Agency like the CHP or DOJ would consider it an insult to be lumped under the heading of 'Local Agency.' [Yes, even in Law Enforcement Agencies men find a way to slip in the argument about size.]

To understand the primary differences between the different agencies, such as California Highway Patrol, Los Angeles County Sheriff's Department, New York Police Department, or the Federal Bureau of Investigation, we need to look at what their primary functions are.

Local Agencies

Responsibilities of Local Agencies

City Police Officers (Cops): Enforce all state and local statues within the boundaries of their city limits.

County Sheriff and their Deputies (Deputies): Maintain county jails, incarceration and protect prisoners, transport prisoners to and from court, ensure security of courts, enforce all state and local statutes in unincorporated county areas, contract law enforcement services. (A City can pay the Sheriff

Department to provide law enforcement for their City).

CHP/State Troopers (State): Respond to all traffic related issues on state highways, enforce all state statutes as they relate to traffic, promote the safe and efficient flow of traffic, ensure safety and security of state buildings and property, assist allied agencies, and respond to all large scale emergency incidents.

California Department of Justice, Division of Law Enforcement/State Police (State): Conduct investigations in the areas of narcotic and criminal activities, financial and medical fraud, and elder abuse; enforce state gambling and firearms laws and regulations, perform work in the forensic sciences, training and education; serve on special task forces; and manage and staff the California Witness Relocation & Protection Program, Sexual Predator Apprehension Team (SPAT), Unsolved Violent Crime Program, Clandestine Laboratory Enforcement.

Jurisdiction of Local Agencies

In states like Nevada where they have a strong State Police (Department of Public Services DPS), the Sheriff usually has less power. I don't mean less Peace Officer powers. I'm referring to the inability to empire build by grabbing a larger share of Federal monies. Think about it, would you, as a Federal Agency, rather deal with one Agency head for information or funding regarding crime and enforcement issues within a state or… would you care to negotiate several different county agencies heads?

A true no brainer. The more Chiefs you deal with the more headaches, er, I mean personalities you have to navigate.

Listed above are the primary functions of the Agencies listed. That's not to say the City Police Department can't have a jail facility, which they oftentimes do. I simply listed the minimum functions required of each Agency. Statewide means they are tasked with enforcement throughout the state. Same applies with county wide and city wide. I'm not saying they can't do more or travel outside their boundaries to enforce laws.

In the State of California, all Peace Officers' Powers, whether they are to work State, County or City Jurisdictions, are granted by the State and therefore the officers can exercise their powers anywhere in the state. The same is true for most states. What I have listed are primary duties. For instance, the Los Angeles Police Department (LAPD) can enforce laws in San Diego, but they are paid by the City of Los Angeles. The City Manager, Mayor and Chief of Police will expect a nexus to Los Angeles lest they scream why are we paying you to clean up San Diego.

Outside of the State of California, Cal-DOJ, Los Angeles Sheriff Department (LASD) and LAPD have no authority to arrest, unless of course, the officer is a member of a Federal Task Force. I will get into Task Forces in a bit.

When a patrol officer/deputy wants to become an Investigator (Investigator is synonymous with Detective for a lot of Departments) the smart ones take classes and demonstrate how they are self-motivated and willing to go the extra mile. Supervisors are always watching and base many decisions on field statistics, attitude, education and well, attitude.

Attitude is *that* important. As is a willingness to learn and listen.

Next, the officer/deputy submits an application for the position. The application could be a simple memo or some other Agency form. Then, depending on the Agency, the applicant may have to go through a testing and interview process or wait for Admin to review the files of all the potential candidates.

Some Agencies rotate patrol officers into and out of Detective positions. They set a time limit for the position, usually two to three years, and then the officer is rotated back to patrol. Other Departments treat the Detective position as a promotion. Once earned, unless demoted, an officer can stay in that position for an entire career if desired.

Rank Structure

DOJ	CHP	LASD	LAPD
	Officer	Deputy	Officer
Special Agent			Detective
	Sergeant	Sergeant	Sergeant
Special Agent Supervisor	Lieutenant	Lieutenant	Lieutenant
Special Agent in Charge	Captain	Captain	Captain
Assistant Chief	Assistant Chief	Commander	Commander
Chief	Chief	Chief	
	Assistant Commissioner	Assistant Sheriff	Deputy Chief
Deputy Director	Deputy Commissioner	Undersheriff	
Director			Chief (Appointed)
Attorney General (Elected)	Commissioner (Appointed)	Sheriff (Elected)	Board of Police Commissioners (Appointed)

The above table lists California Agency's Rank structure from lowest to highest. Reading from left to right is how each rank corresponds to the other agencies.

Federal Agencies

Federal Agents are tasked with enforcing Federal Laws. These Agents do not have authority to enforce state or local statute unless they obtain written permission (which in essence grants them local authority) from the Sheriff or the Chief of Police in the Jurisdiction they are working. In order to gain semi-permanent State powers of arrest, the Federal Agent must be a member of a State or local Task Force.

This website http://www.cga.ct.gov/2010/rpt/2010-R-0042.htm breaks down what types of powers have been granted to Federal Agents in forty-three states. As far as granting Federal Agents any type of Peace Officer Powers, California is one of the most restrictive states.

In reverse, for State and Local Law Enforcement to have the ability to enforce Federal Law, they must be granted Federal Powers from the U.S. Marshalls Service. Again, it would not be blanket powers shared by the entire department or county but rather granted on a case by case basis for a specific individual while they served on a Task Force.

ATF (Bureau of Alcohol, Tobacco, Firearms and Explosives) Federal: Enforce Federal Firearm Statutes, Investigate Arson and Bombings that are not terrorist related actions. The Boston Marathon Bombings were terrorist related, a woman blowing up her no good cheatin' husband's car with him inside, is not.

DEA (Drug Enforcement Administration) National &International: Investigate Major Violators of Controlled Substance Laws operating at the Interstate and International levels, Asset Forfeiture, Diversion, Money Laundering, Southwest Border Initiative, State & Local Task Forces, Foreign Cooperative Investigations, Drug Intelligence.

FBI (Federal Bureau of Investigation) National & International: Enforce Federal Laws and Statutes covering Domestic & International Terrorism, Counter Espionage, Cyber Crime, Corruption, Civil Rights Organized Crime/Drugs, Major Thefts, Violent Crime, White-Collar Crime.

ICE (U.S. Immigration and Customs Enforcement) National & International: Protect Security of the American People and Homeland, Child Exploitations, Human Trafficking, National Security, Smuggling.

CIA (Central Intelligence Agency) Predominately International: Has **NO** Law Enforcement Function, Independent Agency that provides National Security intelligence for senior U.S. Policy Makers, Investigates Foreign Nationals only, and Prohibited from gathering Intel on U.S. Persons no matter where they are located.

NSA/CSS (National Security Agency/Central Security Service) National & International: Collect Foreign Intel from Communication and Info Systems anywhere in world, Prevent Unauthorized access to classified or sensitive National Security Intelligence or Information Systems, Responsible for Security of National Security Information Systems.

With the passage of the Homeland Security Act of 2002, several agencies dealing with immigration, customs, transportation, national security and border security were reorganized, reconfigured or simply disbanded. Customs & Border Protection, Citizenship & Immigration Services, U.S. Coast Guard, Federal Emergency Management, ICE, U.S. Secret Service, Transportation Security Administration and several other agencies were placed under the newly created **Department of Homeland Security (DHS)**. For more information on DHS, check out their Organizational Chart (http://www.dhs.gov/xlibrary/assets/dhs-orgchart.pdf).

It's a sad and sorry truth, but most Federal Agencies do not talk or share information. Think of siblings trying to prove to a parent who is the more worthwhile child. Anyone with brothers or sisters or both knows what I mean. You withhold a critical piece of information and sit back, watching and waiting for your rival to fall flat on their face. Well the same goes for Federal Agencies. To be fair, State and Local Agencies aren't much better.

Task Forces

The most basic definition of a Task Force is: Various Agencies at any level (Local/State and Federal or any combination thereof) joining together, pooling resources and personnel in a joint effort with a common Law Enforcement goal.

When a Task Force is formed, a Memorandum of Understanding (MOU) is created and signed by the various agencies joining the Task Force. The MOU designates who is in charge of the Task Force and it also appoints an Oversight Committee that usually consists of the Chief of Police (or his Designee) of every agency participating on the Task Force. The MOU, once signed, is basically a contract of who is in charge, how things will be run, who pays for what and how much money each agency receives from any resulting asset forfeiture.

The basic principal behind Law Enforcement Task Forces: The Host Agency (usually the Agency Creating the Task Force) wants bodies and control while moving forward toward solving a community dilemma. The other Agencies that get involved with a Task Force want something out of their participation, too.

Most often, officers on patrol are the best initiators of high yield/significant cases. Patrol Cops usually work the same beats (areas) daily. They know those neighborhoods and its citizens. This makes it easier for Patrol to notice people and/or vehicles out of place or simply acting out of character. People who commit crimes are usually either in a hurry or simply feel most laws don't apply to them. Patrol Officers make a lot of warrant, drug and weapon arrests by stopping someone for a simple traffic violation like speeding or running a red light or stop sign.

Once that person is booked into the jail facility, a Station Detective would interview and dig, possibly unearthing a major drug ring or some other type of crime syndicate. The biggest advantage County and Local Agencies have on State Agencies like the California Department of Justice and all the Federal Agencies are their patrol cars.

Patrol Officers have the pulse beat of their area. Patrol is the one who notices more crime in any specific area, hot spots, trends, and they usually know, or are told, who's up to what. This information, when passed on to Investigators, accounts for a good deal of large seizures.

Working as a Special Agent for the California Department of Justice (CA-DOJ), we didn't have Patrol Officers to generate cases for us. Most of the investigations I worked were cases developed by prior arrests. What I mean is, once we arrested someone for Crime A, in order to get a reduced sentence they had to point us in the direction of another crook who was at or above their level. Usually, we tried to get our in-custody crook to give us their supplier. We wanted to work up the supply ladder, not down.

Some crooks bargain and gave up anyone and everyone they could think of, usually starting with their customers. Others refuse to even give their real name. The problem with this method of generating cases is that eventually leads dry up. So to pull in fresh resources and enhance the ever important manpower issues, CA-DOJ put in place a lot of Task Forces which were created to enhance enforcement of specific laws in targets areas of the State.

For instance, upon my arrival in Riverside, CA, I was assigned to IECLTF (Inland Empire Clandestine Laboratory Task Force). My team worked Clandestine Methamphetamine (Meth) Labs. We had several Police Departments, Sheriff Departments and Federal Agencies on the Task Force.

The reason all those agencies were involved came down to money. Clan Lab clean up was prohibitively expensive, averaging $5,000 per lab, but could be much more due to contamination and damage to the structure or environment. If an Agency was a member of IECLTF and they located a Lab in their city, CA-DOJ would pay for the cleanup. CA-DOJ received extra bodies for case work, the Cities and Counties saved a bundle in lab clean up costs. A win-win for both sides.

A few months after I arrived, Riverside Bureau of Narcotic Enforcement (BNE) started INCA (Inland CrackDown Allied Task Force). CrackDown was a state mandated program at its inception in 1990. INCA investigated Colombian and Mexican Drug Traffickers and Money Launderers. INCA started off slow but as we began making large seizures of both cocaine and money, the team grew. During my time with INCA, my team seized well over ten tons of cocaine and over ten million dollars in cash.

Yes, you read that right. Over ten million in _cash_.

In addition to receiving a portion of the proceeds from asset forfeiture, any Agency member of INCA had the ability to sign up their informants under the INCA pay scale. Most local Agencies didn't have the resources to pay their informants much money. The deeper State and Federal pockets were added motivation for Departments to join State and Federal Task Forces.

In my opinion, the greatest asset of being on a Task Force is every Agency involved brings something unique and important to the team. All aspects of a case can be covered and investigated. Need a watch put out for a suspect known to cross the border? Ask Frank, he works for ICE (Immigration and Custom Enforcement). Want to have a shipment intercepted in New Jersey? Ralph is with DEA (Drug Enforcement Agency) I bet he can get an East Coast Team. Your suspect has terrorist ties, pass that over to Tim with the FBI (Federal Bureau of Investigation).

Do agents and officers on Task Forces pass off cases like that? Yes, pretty much. See, the initiating officer gets to keep their hand in or even retains the case. The person with the expertise helps them to get what they need.

You know how I hinted at non-cooperation between Agencies? Well, an unintended by product of Task Forces ended up being a newfound level of cooperation. If DEA, FBI or CA-DOJ is not playing nice, you have their person on the Task Force go deal with the problem. It's easy to say no or ignore an outside Agency, not so much to one of your own.

When I worked on INCA, the cases we investigated sometimes led us to other states or even across the Mexican Border. Depending on the case, the Case Agent (Investigator in charge of an investigation) might travel to that state for follow-up. Sometimes the only way to get the information was to call the jurisdiction where information was needed. Usually, due to time constraints, budget and red tape, travel outside the State/U.S. was discouraged or flat out denied.

During one of my INCA cases, we lost our crook. Okay – politically correct dictates I should say suspect. Every cop, amongst themselves, calls them crooks or other highly unflattering terms. This one was a multi-kilo dealing Mexican Cowboy. Anyway, per my informant, my crook was traveling out-of-state to oversee a dope deal.

> **Something To Think About (STTA):** Mexican Cocaine Traffickers were called Cowboys because of their pennant for carrying flashy weapons – like pearl handled revolvers or nickel plated .45s. They often sported large white or light colored cowboy hats and usually had matching cowboy boots. The strongest reason for the 'cowboy' nickname was their strong propensity to get into shootouts. Seems Mexican Cocaine Traffickers thought it was cool to go out in a blaze of glory. That or they watched too many westerns and thought the white hat meant they would win any gun battle.

Through my investigation of this particular Mexican Cowboy, I identified a couple of out-of-state addresses where my crook might settle. The locations could have been a stash pad (houses that are virtually empty except for a mattress to sleep on and large amounts narcotics stored throughout the house) or simply a residence of a co-conspirator. When I talk about Narcotic Investigations, I will get into how another jurisdiction's seizure of drugs made my case stronger.

For all of the out-of-state locations connected to my crook, I called each of the local police departments' Investigation Bureaus to request assistance. On my first call, I was put on hold and subsequently forgotten. After waiting about fifteen minutes, I hung up and called back, asking for the Watch Commander (WC) or supervisor on duty.

When transferred, I identified myself and I told the WC generics about the case I was working, what I needed and then asked for assistance. He transferred me to an investigator who, after I gave him the address, asked if I realized how far the area I wanted him to drive to was from his office. Okay, it's thirty miles from his desk, that's still 1,100 closer than it was to mine. It's never pretty when anyone whines, but coming from a grown man, it's downright unsettling.

I asked if they (his department) had a narcotics team. Based on his tone of voice, I knew I would not be receiving anything but lip service. Mr. Whiny told me no, all of the narcotics cases were worked by a HIDTA Group in another city. I asked for their phone number. He didn't know it and couldn't be bothered to find it. Yeah, I had about as much luck getting him to check my crook's address as I did growing a third ear.

But he gave me something more, so I didn't ask to be transferred back to his supervisor. Instead, I called Jim. My Agency's Agent in HIDTA Group 50, gave him my crook's address and told him what I needed. Jim said he'd locate the nearest HIDTA Group to my target and pass along the basics of my case and my contact info. He didn't promise anything but said I should get a phone call in a day or two.

Within a few hours I was contacted by Craig who went over the case with me and how I wanted his end of the investigation to go. I gave him all of the background information I had on the organization expanding their 'business operations' to his back yard and brought him up to speed on how they worked. When Craig asked me what I wanted him to do, I told him I had intel my crook was back there doing a multi-kilo deal. If Craig and his team could develop enough PC (Probable Cause) on their own to hit (serve a search warrant) any of the locations, I'd appreciate copies of any info or reports generated. I could hear the smile in Craig's voice as he agreed.

The happiness in Craig's voice let me know he understood I had basically handed him a treasure map with a huge X on it. Yes, he had to do some work to reach the 'treasure', but at least he knew right where to find it. Add to that the only thing I asked for in return was copies of his reports and case files.

Craig and his team surveilled the location for less than a week and were able to build enough probable cause for a warrant. When they hit the house, Eureka! A stash pad with about 400 kilograms of cocaine.

Funny, I hadn't thought about using Jim until Mr. Whiny said HIDTA.

Who knew you could mine a Jim in a Whine field.

- Have you given your Law Enforcement Officer (LEO) the best Law Enforcement career to keep your story on track?

Chapter Two

Surveillance
Electronic vs. Physical

Most investigations are started because someone somewhere sees something suspicious or events that are downright illegal. Law Enforcement uses surveillance as an investigative tool to gather the intelligence and evidence needed to convict.

Electronic Surveillance

Communication Intercepts: (AKA Wire Intercepts, AKA Wiretaps, AKA Title III Investigations, AKA Title III) In 1967, Katz vs. United States, the United States Supreme Court ruled telephone communications were protected under the Fourth Amendment of the United States Constitution. Wiretaps were not again legal until 1968 when Congress passed Title III.

Title III allows States to have their own communication intercept laws as long as they meet minimum Federal guidelines. State wiretap laws usually grossly exceed the Federal guidelines, restriction wise.

Most states only require one person within the conversation to give consent or know taping is occurring for the recording to be legal. California, Connecticut, Florida, Illinois, Maryland, Massachusetts, Michigan, Montana, Nevada, New Hampshire, Pennsylvania and Washington require all parties to the conversation give their consent for the recording to be legal. In those States anything else is considered wiretapping and completely illegal.

Electronic eavesdropping (listening in on a conversation by using enhancements) is also considered wiretapping.

<u>**Something To Think About (STTA):**</u> The reason communication intercepts are called wiretaps is because – back in the day – the telephone company had to go out to the telephone switch box (usually located close to the suspect's location) and 'tap' into a wire that led to the crook's telephone. With the advent of digital communications it's much easier to monitor communications. Today it's simply a matter of digitally routing or having the information forwarded to a second location, but the term Wiretap still remains.

Federal (Title III) vs. State Wiretap Law: Title III – Federal Wiretaps can be authorized for a long list of serious crimes –

(http://www.law.cornell.edu/uscode/uscode18/usc_sec
_18_00002516----000-.html).

States are limited to specific crimes they can
investigate while utilizing a wiretap:

- A narcotics investigation involving specific
  drugs: Cocaine, heroin, methamphetamine,
  PCP, or their precursors or analogs. (There is
  a minimum amount of ten gallons or three
  pounds of narcotics that must be involved
  for the case to be considered wiretap
  worthy.)
- Narcotic money laundering (the amount
  must be over $100,000)
- Murder or solicitation to commit murder
- Kidnapping
- Destructive device, felony violation of penal
  code 186.22, weapons of mass destruction
- An attempt or conspiracy to commit any of
  the above

Wire Taps are complicated and not just because of the
equipment and technology needed to effectively
gather the information, but due in large part to the
public's expectation of privacy. No court or Agency
says: "Hmm I wonder what the Gambino family is
doing? Wake Judge Smith. He owes me a favor. I want
a tap on all their phones up and running by

tomorrow." When I hear or read dialogue like that, I laugh myself silly.

By both State and Federal standards the guidelines for writing a Communication Intercept Warrant are tough. Wiretaps are not an initiating tool, they are considered the last item ever pulled out of a cop's investigative arsenal. The affidavit used to get the warrant must show officers exhausted every other avenue of investigation before turning to wire taps.

Something To Think About (STTA): When either a Federal or State wire intercept is approved it is given a thirty day time frame for operation. Federal law requires a report be filed with the judge every ten days updating and giving the progress report of the information obtained and more importantly a reason why the wiretap should continue another ten days. California law requires case updates be filed every six days.

Privileged Communications

It's important to mention there are privileged communications that should not be arbitrarily monitored. They are:

- Attorney/Client
- Doctor/Patient
- Clergyman/Parishioner
- Psychotherapist/Patient
- Husband/Wife

If one of the above listed communications is intercepted, the recorded communication must be shut off for a minimum of two minutes. After a complete two minutes passes the officer/agent can again turn on the recording device for up to thirty seconds to determine the nature of the communications. If it is determined to still be a privileged communication then the recording device must once again be switched off for two full minutes. The officer/agent is required to repeat the on thirty seconds/off for two minutes until it is either determined the communication is no longer privileged or someone hangs up.

Now that you know the logistics of obtaining a wiretap, let's get into the logistics of the wireroom setup. The information being intercepted is considered sensitive, so a separate room with a locking door is required to house all communication intercept equipment. There is a wireroom log that everyone entering and leaving must sign.

A lot of times civilian personnel are hired to listen to and transcribe the voice recordings. Most of our translators spoke multiple languages. Translators cannot be inside the wire room without Law Enforcement supervision.

Before the switch is flipped and the wire intercept is made active everyone, and I do mean *everyone*, who is to work inside the wire room must be sworn in by either the Assistant United States Attorney (AUSA) or the Deputy District Attorney (DDA) supervising the case.

Something To Think About (STTA): The average wire tap costs approximately $60,000 a month to run.

Every bit of information seized or intercepted during a Title III is considered confidential information and not to be accessed by anyone other than those people sworn onto the case. Failure to keep the wire room clear of nonessential personnel or failure to keep all wire information in the wire room can result in suppression of all conversations intercepted and immediate termination of the wiretap.

Trust me, nobody wants the wire terminated or suppressed, especially considering the time and expense of running one.

Pen Registers: A device that registers the numbers dialed out on a telephone.

Trap and Trace: A method of trapping all incoming telephone calls to a specific number and tracing them back to their origins. This does include gathering information on telephone numbers that display blocked or otherwise unavailable.

Tracking Devices: GPS and Lo-Jack type devices are the type of devices I am talking about. Believe it or not, most Lo-Jack type of equipment can be stuck to the bottom of a vehicle in less than five minutes. The only problem is a search warrant is required if the vehicle is parked in a private garage. Once a vehicle is on private property, out of view, there is that dastardly expectation of privacy that kicks in. Without a warrant, any buildings or locations identified solely from the tracking device are not admissible in court. This means, tracking devices by themselves are only good for supplementing moving surveillances. Because there is no expectation of privacy as the vehicle is traversing a public street.

Life tracking (trying to figure out the suspects patterns and locations without physically having eyes on the target), is much easier with a warrant. Periodically the tracker can be accessed to see if the suspect is moving (like in the middle of the night when no one else is around and our suspect gets active). Trackers also help to establish movement patterns – do we need to have a physical surveillance in place at dawn break? Or are they night Owls?

Computers: Everything you do on your computer can be recreated. Erasing data, photos and files only makes it a little more difficult and/or time consuming to retrieve the information. The only guarantee your deleted information cannot be accessed is to reformat and stamp the hard drive. I've worked with people who were absolute geniuses at retrieving information from supposed 'wiped' hard drives.

The internet is much worse when it comes to little or no security as far as keeping your information solely to your computer. On the internet it's not only Law Enforcement tracking and/or monitoring your information, it's hackers and people who design and build websites.

In fact, Law Enforcement is having a real rough time intercepting, let alone monitoring, communications over the internet. Peer-to-peer software, VoIP and encryption have thwarted all of Law Enforcement efforts at electronic eavesdropping. Until either backdoor or descrambling equipment can be developed, some areas of electronic communication are safe from monitoring. Well, as long as you don't count some No-Named-Black-Ops Agency. ;-}

The government can track most email messages and identify, in most instances and with a lot of help from the carrier, the location and/or origin of a message. When I worked Sexual Predators my first Traveler/Child Pornography Case (I will go into Traveler Cases in Chapter Four) came from Wyoming.

An on-line sexual predator was attempting to get what he thought was a twelve year old girl (that was in fact a Special Agent (Fred) with the Wyoming Attorney General's Division of Criminal Investigation) to take nude, provocative photos of herself and send them to him. This predator had already transmitted several child pornography photos to the 'little girl'.

When Fred contacted me he provided me with everything I needed to make a case against the predator he had been 'chatting' with on the internet. Fred gave me not only the IP address of the predator, he also gave me the physical address (Palm Springs, California) as well. The reason I was given the case was, although new to the Sexual Predator Team, I had worked for two years in Palm Springs on a Narcotics Task Force.

Just like a telephone number, every computer connected to the internet is assigned a unique number. That number, the IP (Internet Protocol) address, identifies the physical location and the subscriber of the internet services. My job was to gather all the physical evidence and tie it to the IP address and a specific person. Not nearly as hard as it sounds, especially with my prior Law Enforcement contacts in the area. Once I gathered all the necessary information and married it with the information from the Wyoming Attorney General's Office, which included transcripts of conversations and copies of photos and movies (provided by the email carrier) both sent and received between the two email addresses, I obtained a search warrant.

Basically, it was a mud pie recipe type case. Easy procedural wise, emotionally it was a very difficult case. In a future book I will tackle the emotional toll the job of Law Enforcement has on those who 'Protect and Serve'.

Pole Cameras: Are just that. Cameras that usually sit on a pole. Of course they are disguised as birds, or sneakers on a string. Just Kidding. Pole cameras are usually housed inside the round transformer casings or overhead street lights. The camera can be remote activated, but for surveillance is usually a static camera.

Physical Surveillance

Most physical surveillances are moving surveillances.

Fixed surveillance: Where the point (person or camera that has an unfettered view of the item or person being watched) stays in one place and calls out all movement. As you can guess, fixed points are static and therefore once the target leaves the area—unless there is a surveillance team nearby—the subject is off to do his bad stuffs with no witnesses.

Moving surveillance: Consists of actively following someone on foot, by car, from a fixed wing airplane or helicopter, train, boat or anything else some clever minded individual comes up with to keep tabs on the crook/suspect.

Air Surveillance: Believe it or not there are several drawbacks with air surveillance. From the air buildings, trees, overhangs can block the view of the 'eye-in-the-sky.' Air Space is another drawback. Different airports have different restrictions, not to mention frequencies, for their airspace. It's easy to be pulled off point when the area the surveillance is entering has several airports. Some areas gave us a 500 foot ceiling (we could not fly higher than 500 ft) in others we couldn't fly below 2,000 feet. Both played havoc on my skills as an observer during a moving surveillance.

I was a helicopter observer for INCA for a short period of time. The assignment was fun, but difficult. My job entailed not losing sight of the vehicle while directing ground units to the suspect's location as I kept track of the direction of travel while attempting to figure out the street names. Because of line-of-sight communications, I heard every conversation (even those from units three cities over) and was often asked to relay messages. I never signed up to be a dispatcher.

Hell, one of my fellow Agents blamed me for his traffic collision. The ground team was following around a major narcotics dealer who drove erratically and dangerously in order to figure out if he was being followed (called counter-surveillance driving or cleaning his tail). He was also good at finding and parking under awnings and over passes (this was his attempt at shaking any potential air surveillance) so I had to really watch and time where he was and anticipate where he should be when he drove under a bridge or overpass.

The ground team's job was to feed me the street names so I could announce where the suspect was. This crook's driving kept the ground crew back so I had no street names and did my best to figure them out. The crook landed (stopped) at a warehouse after an exorbitant amount of counter-surveillance driving (even for him), which lead us all to believe it was the storage location of his narcotics. AKA, a very important location.

Being I was the only one who saw where he went, it was up to me to direct the ground troops to his location. I spotted one of my ground team and attempted to direct them in. All I asked Robert was the name of the major (cop slang for a large street) directly behind him. Robert made an abrupt U-turn and smashed into a civilian car. So his crash was my fault – riiiight.

The location did in fact turn out to be the Crook's stash pad and once the warrant was signed we seized a few hundred kilograms of cocaine.

Ground Surveillance: The most effective moving surveillance team has five to seven cars. Those cars should be all makes and models. Flashy cars simply draw attention to the driver and have the potential to get easily 'burned' (identified and then looked for). The goal of surveillance is to watch someone's activities without being noticed.

The more cars, the easier it is to change the point (lead vehicle) right behind the target. The same car might follow a suspect from Sacramento to San Diego – leap frogging – but once he gets close to his destination, it looks strange to have a Silver Ford Taurus behind him to his door step. The hardest thing about surveillance is driving like a normal car while anticipating what your target will do and where that target will go.

Optimally, if the team is lucky enough to have a helicopter, your surveillance is usually a lot easier. Both the ground team and the helicopter play to each other's strengths and make the combination of the two surveillances pretty successful.

Something To Think About (STTA): Female Agents oft times are frequently called on to follow a suspect on foot into malls, grocery stores, restaurants etc. Women cops are still greatly overlooked by criminals. I could and would go make a phone call on a phone right next to a suspect in order to try and overhear his conversation and to 'mark his phone' when he was done. I was never 'made'.

The purpose of a surveillance team is to gather enough probable cause to obtain search warrants. To this end, every surveillance team had a note taker (Scribe) assigned daily. The Scribe took all of the observations along with who saw what and where for the entire team for the full day. All team members were asked to jot down their notes in case the Scribe missed something. Each day one of the surveillance team members was selected to be the Scribe.

At the end of the day there would be a field debriefing where everything about the surveillance was discussed. What when wrong? What went right? This was also the time the Scribe filled in any gaps inside his notes. The Scribe would then create a report from the daily observations. These reports were used to develop probable cause for search warrants and/or arrests.

When I was sent to the High Impact Drug Trafficking Area (HIDTA) Task Force, it was not a place I wanted to be. At that time, HIDTA Group 50 didn't have a good reputation, some Agents called that team an embarrassment. I had put a request in to be considered for a Regional Narcotics Task Force. IRNET (Inland Regional Narcotics Enforcement Team) was another highly active and successful Task Force. I was looking to enhance my surveillance and investigative skills not diminish them. But instead, my request was ignored, 'Needs of the Department' was invoked and I was shanghaied, I mean sent to HIDTA.

I was told the main reasons I was selected as the one to be sent to HIDTA were my field and case making experience in addition to my strong personality. My then supervisors confirmed the HIDTA Group I was being sent to was off track. They were investigating street level crimes when they were supposed to be targeting major traffickers.

Supposedly because of my investigative and surveillance experience, they expected me to make a difference. Awkward feeling, having smoke blown up your butt. My first day was horrible. Inside the office there were two different factions who barely spoke to each other. Surveillance was a total nightmare. Task Force Officers (TFOs) were openly cussing each other out over the radio. Two people took point and continually 'walked over' (talking on the radio at the same time another is transmitting, the result is an incoherent garbled mess) each other.

Because of all that nonsense we were 'burned' (the target recognized he was under surveillance and, even worse, identified who was following him) and then to top off our shame, we lost the suspect. Of course, more cussing over the radio ensued. Talk about completely unprofessional.

I asked where the debriefing was going to be. I had a few things I needed to get off my chest. I could really care less about the notes at this point I wanted a platform to talk about **Teamwork**.

Surveillance debriefings are usually held in the field immediately following the end of the operation, not only for learning purposes but to assist the person taking the field notes that day. Field notes are a running commentary on all the actions the suspect did that day. Everything is documented and put into the case file. Sometimes it's not until days or weeks later that the suspect visiting a specific house becomes clear or important. Often times targets do their best to compartmentalize their organization in an attempt to protect their 'assets' from Law Enforcement or other criminals so they have usually have secondary stash pads or otherwise 'safe locations' that they rarely visit or tell others about.

The response I received: The team didn't have debriefings.

Yep, and it showed.

Becoming a unified team took time and the help of two Orange County Sheriff Deputies fresh off another surveillance team. Between us, we bullied, cajoled and embarrassed our way to becoming a fully functioning, elite surveillance team. Before I left HIDTA Group 50, our team was not only primarily working and directing wire investigations, my team had received the highest award given out by the Drug Enforcement Administration (DEA) The Administrators Award.

So I was fortunate enough to be on a team that went from being burned to a cohesive team that earned the highest award. Solid teamwork makes or breaks an investigation.

– In your story is the main Law Enforcement Officer (LEO) a loner or does he/she play well with others?

Chapter Three

Undercover Operations, Narcotic Investigations, Money Laundering & Informants

<u>Undercover Operations</u>

Basically every police investigation where the evidence is collected by individuals (LEO's or Informants) who do not identify themselves as Law Enforcement or agents for Law Enforcement is an undercover (U/C) operation.

Narcotics Investigations leads the way as far as the number and complexity of U/C Operations. In Chapter Four I go over Sex crimes and Homicide. Traveler cases and Murder for Hire will have to wait until that Chapter.

Not every officer can operate effectively undercover. The ability to story tell and role play is a major criteria for the U/C. If you cannot convince a crook that you, too, are a well… a crook, then the investigation is over before it ever really began. The goal of an U/C operation is to get the suspect to conduct or facilitate illegal activities where they can be witnessed or recorded.

My first stint U/C was in the hood – a heavily African-American area of San Bernardino, California. I knew what my activities were to be that night, so I have no excuse for dressing like a preppy college student. I wore severely pressed and starched stone washed jeans, a white Triple A – baseball sweatshirt with orange and blue highlights. My turtle neck shirt was matching orange and my shoes were the crowd pleasing white sneakers.

Looking back, I cringe at my attire. When I showed up for briefing before the operation I was razzed to no end. At the time I didn't have a change of clothes nor did I have time to run out and purchase new, subdued clothes to wear. Because I looked so preppie, I was sure I would be made (identified) as a Narc (undercover narcotics officer) and make no illicit drug purchases that evening.

During the briefing all three of us new CA-DOJ agents were partnered with veteran San Bernardino Police Department U/C Narcotic Investigators. The three U/C teams were each assigned a cover team and an arrest team. The arrest and cover teams would go into an area and locate potential drug dealers and set up around them. Once ready, they'd call in the U/C team.

We (the U/C team) would enter the area, contact the suspect and attempt to make a buy. If the buy was made, we had a prearranged physical bust signal as well as a verbal one. As soon as possible, we radioed description of the person(s) we bought from. The arrest team would wait until we left the area (followed by the cover team) before they swooped in and detained and/or arrested all parties to the crime.

Each team was given a couple hundred dollars of 'buy' money. The 'buy' money was photocopied and the serial numbers recorded. If found in the subject's possession, this was additional evidence that the subject arrested was the one who sold the U/C the narcotics.

The Undercover buy teams were broken down into two white males, two Hispanic males and two black females. (Hey not my idea – I was only there for the cookies). I was partnered with Daisy, a veteran officer with the San Bernardino Police Department. She told me not to worry about my clothes. In fact she bet the other teams going out we (she and I) would make the most U/C buys that evening. Nothing brings a group of cops alive like a challenge. Bets for breakfast and bragging rights were quickly made.

Al and Sandoval, the Hispanic males, snatched up a rusted, lowered, old school Chevy Monte Carlo that San Bernardino Police Department dragged out for buy operations. KR and Steve used another beater (really old, clunker looking car). Daisy and I were given a brand new compact rental car. Talk about trying to stack the odds in their favor, sheez.

With there being three U/C teams going out, none of the undercover officers wore wires. All of us – per department policy – were armed, carrying handcuffs and a spare, fully loaded gun magazine. Our male counterparts had police radios mounted and hidden in their cars and handheld radios. Daisy and I were given one hand held radio. Car mounted radios have a much greater range for transmissions.

Once in the car with Daisy, she went over the area. She told me she and I were the only female, black U/C's as far as she knew of throughout the Inland Empire (San Bernardino and Riverside Counties). She was pretty sure no local crooks had ever been approached by two black women and been arrested. So short of wearing a police uniform, she believed every drug dealer we approached would be basically throwing narcotics at us.

She was right. We not only made the most narcotic purchases, we bought narcotics from two dealers they had not been able to get close to before. Daisy stayed in the car on both occasions because she was concerned the dealers might recognize her.

Me with my preppy clothes, and so help me – for some unknown reason I began speaking with an English accent (at least it felt that way) "Pardon me, I would like to purchase one gram of your finest Cocaine. Is it fresh today?" – made the buys.

When I walked up to Mr. Big Deal Dope Dealer, he looked at me, sized me up and asked if I was a cop. My hands started shaking (I was terrified of blowing it) and I tried to laugh it off and asked him if I looked like a cop. He scowled and said that's not what he asked. So I lied and denied being a cop as I tried to recall what case law made it okay to use trickery and deceit to get the job done.

Something To Think About (STTA): Somewhere, someone started a rumor that if asked a cop must always tell the truth and identify themselves. Not true. There is even a U.S Supreme Court ruling upholding the use of Trickery & Deceit by Law Enforcement Officers:

- Officers can lie and say – 'Your partner in crime has confessed and implicated you in the crime.' Per the Supreme Court: False assertions are permissible.

- Props are also okay as long as the officer does not assert them to be evidence.

- There are limitations.

- Investigators cannot use any methods that might shock the conscience such as impersonating an attorney or clergy man to get a confession.

- Fabricating evidence is not a permissible part of trickery and deceit.

Entrapment

Entrapment is when an officer persuades or induces a person to commit a crime they had no previous intention of committing. The gauge of whether it is entrapment or not is measured by what a reasonable and innocent person would do?

As I continued to shake, he held his hand out for my money. Before I handed it to him I pulled the money back toward me and asked if he was going to rip me off. At this point I was quite distracted. I was trying to remember how to breathe and doing my best not to puke all over him. I so wanted to make the buy and knew I had to give up the money but was worried he'd take off with it. Then I'd be laughed at for not only not making the buy, but for fronting (give up money without getting the product) and losing Departmental cash.

Yes, all of my fear and nervousness had nothing to do with concern over my physical safety. Between cops, image is everything. I was terrified of screwing up publicly in front of my peers.

Next thing I knew, Mr. Big Deal Dope Dealer smiled and his face softened. He produced his entire stash of rock cocaine and took his time selecting a large, pretty rock. Dope Dealers don't normally show off their entire stash of narcotics. I passed some kind of test and he deemed me harmless. He was actually taking pity on me.

I remember thinking, awww how nice – didn't stop me from giving the bust signal.

That was my first U/C narcotics purchase.

There are many different types of narcotic operations. As with anything, a narcotic operation is limited only by the imagination and foresight of the investigator.

Street Buy Program: This is where an area or type of drug is usually targeted and purchased. My first buy was part of a Street Buy Program. Another type of Street Buy Program is one where the Undercover (U/C) Officers/ or Agents can be 'set-up' on a street corner and they 'sling' (sell) dope to vehicles that pull up. In that instance the cover team stays close to the U/C's and the chase and arrest team follow the person who purchased the narcotics.

There are many variations to the Street Buy Program. One time, I was put in a vehicle that was completely wired with a camera that filmed and recorded every buy I made.

Buy – Bust: A single purchase of narcotics. Immediately following the exchange of money for narcotics a signal is given and the suspect is arrested. Buy-Busts are usually done in hotel rooms, parking lots or a mall. Very dangerous because the crook knows the U/C will be carrying or bringing a large sum of money to the meet.

Buy – Walk: This is a very rare occurrence and it takes a very big criminal (we're talking direct ties to a Cartel type criminal) – and an understanding supervisor – to allow an agent to purchase an amount of narcotics from a suspect and let them leave, un-accosted, with the money.

Something To Think About (STTA): For officer safety reasons, U/C are never to participate in the arrest of the suspect, unless of course he needs to act to prevent the injury of another officer. The U/C spent a lot of time and effort convincing the suspect that he, too, was a crook. If a suspect sees the U/C helping, he (the suspect) might view events as being a rip off. This could cause the suspect to fight back.

High School Buy Programs: A baby faced officer or agent is sent to High School to fit in and buy narcotics or other dangerous drugs. The officer is usually by themselves with little to no back up. For this reason, the U/C must be a full officer at least 21 years old that is selected simply because they look so young. During the program a pair of officers share an apartment while they attend school (usually each officer goes to a different school). Their phones are monitored and they're required to live at the apartment Monday through Friday and no real life family or girlfriends are allowed to visit the apartment. The program usually lasts the whole school year.

Reverse Buy: This is where the U/C is actually selling narcotics for money. During this type of operation – to prove the U/C is not entrapping the suspect – the U/C will usually make the suspect take extraordinary measures to make a purchase. This is also one of the most dangerous U/C operations. By virtue of the U/C having a large quantity of narcotics other crooks never think of the U/C as a cop. What comes quickly to the crooks mind is how they can steal all the drugs and sell them for 100% profit.

Tommy DeLa Rosa, a Fullerton Police Officer working Narcotics, was murdered during just such a narcotics transaction.

Exchange: Instead of money for drugs, the exchange could be weapons for drugs or drugs for weapons, etc.

Informant Buy: An informant is sent (usually followed by a surveillance team) to a location or individual and purchases narcotics. The informant and his vehicle are searched before and immediately after he leaves the suspects location. The searches are to show the only place the informant could have received the drugs was from the suspects.

Narcotic Investigations:

Identify Targets – Based on the information received and using every database known, a complete background is researched on the suspect.

Once a viable target is identified, their name is run through LA CLEAR (for California) and/or the local RISS (Regional Information Sharing Systems) network. RISS has six centers nationwide. California is part of the WSIN (Western States Information Network) Both these data collection programs were created to protect and assist investigators in the field as well as share information. Investigators are told if that target is currently under investigation, if there were any past investigations and who the investigating Agencies were. If the target is already being worked, then both Agencies come together and LA CLEAR or RISS personnel sit in as moderators to decide who has the best case and that Agency gets to work the subject.

Informants that are reliable (trustworthy) or control problems (hard to work with won't follow directions) are also listed in the databases. Before an informant receives one penny from an Agency it has become Standard Operating Procedure (SOP) to run their name and find out what their record is: Reliable or unreliable.

The best safety feature of LA CLEAR is the War Room (place where all in progress undercover law enforcement operations are actively monitored). Whenever a team is doing surveillance, drug buy, drug bust, gang sweep or search warrant that team has to inform the War Room of their operation. This way two surveillance teams don't conflict and two undercover officers working on different teams don't attempt to buy and sell dope from each other. If two teams end up working within five miles of each other, it is deemed a conflict and the Case Agents of each team are notified.

For every investigation there is usually a Case Agent and a co-Case Agent. The Case Agent is the lead investigator and dictates the direction of the case. The co-Case Agent is the Case Agent's right hand and sounding board. If the Case Agent is unavailable the co-Case Agent is in charge.

Usually.

When I was Case Agent I had a hard time releasing the reigns of my case to my co-Case Agent. It boils down to control and trust issues. Hell, one time I was simply the wireroom manager (which automatically made me the Case Agent) on a case my Agency brought to me to develop. Because I was assigned to HIDTA, I wrote and brought my CA-DOJ Lab team up on the Title III Wire Intercept. I stayed in the wireroom while the original Case Agent and Co-Case Agent ran the field surveillance teams.

The whole purpose of a wiretap is a tool of last resort. That means, for whatever reason, law enforcement *can't* investigate the crook through normal methods. U/Cs and CI's are unable to order narcotics from him, physical surveillances don't work or the team continually gets 'burned', members of the target's organization are not willing to tell how the target operates. All other means of investigation have been exhausted. In essence a wiretap comes into play when all other means of investigation have been exhausted.

So, imagine my surprise and total mortification when the field Case Agent called the crook on the recorded wiretapped line to instigate a dope deal. For professional reasons I won't tell you my initial response, but let's simply say it was loud and quite profane. Being able to call up the crook and order a load means there was no need for the wire. Lucky for the field Case Agent, the crook totally blew him off. That didn't alleviate my responsibility to report the incident to the Judge who signed *MY* affidavit not to mention the AUSA (Assistant United States Attorney) that reviewed all my paperwork. That one phone call had the potential of ruining my credibility and give the impression I'd lie by omission to get a wiretap up and running.

Once I spoke with the both the Judge and AUSA, I scheduled an immediate sit-down with the soon to be two *co*-Case-Agents and their Supervisor. I took control of the investigation, my signature on the affidavit meant it was my reputation and credibility that were on the line. I made sure everyone in that meeting understood I wasn't going to sit back and allow damage to either because the case wasn't developing fast enough for them. I also told the former Case Agent that any other calls by him or anyone he put up to the task on the recorded line would result in the wire being shut down.

Most LEOs get emotionally invested in their case and have an issue letting others make decisions that could potentially negatively impact the outcome of the case. I wasn't emotionally attached to this case but, because I was the Affiant on the search warrant, my reputation was tied to the case. I didn't realize that meant anything to me until I envisioned all of my hard work being negated by the thoughtless and careless actions of another.

Evidence Gathering:. This is where information from the wiretap or surveillance creates enough probable cause for a search warrant to be issued. Surveillances can go on for months. Everyday all the information gathered is collected and put in a report. The case is built on all of the daily observations.

Something To Think About (STTA): Definition of a Search Warrant per California Penal Code Section 1523: 'A search warrant is an order in writing, in the name of the people, signed by a magistrate, directed to a peace officer, commanding him or her to search for a person or persons, a thing or things, or personal property, and, in the case of a thing or things or personal property, bring the same before the magistrate.'

In order to obtain a Search Warrant an Officer must prepare a statement (called an Affidavit) which shows enough probable cause (reasonableness) to compel a judge to sign the document making it an order.

If the surveillance team is lucky enough to witness what appears to be a trunk-to-trunk (gun/narcotic) transaction – two people both opening their trunks and transferring items from one trunk to the other, the primary target is allowed to drive away. By letting the primary target leave with a small surveillance team following, the primary target has no idea he was followed to the meet location. He believes he's in the clear because the cops didn't stop him too when he later finds out the person he handed off to was arrested, The second vehicle is stopped, usually by a marked patrol car. If any type of contraband is found in the trunk, that will give investigators enough

Probable Cause (PC) to obtain a search warrant for the primary target's various locations.

In Chapter One, I mentioned how a drug bust in a different jurisdiction enhanced my case—this is that case in point. I gave Craig information and his team went out on a specific target (Max). I gave Craig all of the information I had gathered on Max, how he and his criminal organization operated and locations I had identified as under the control of Max and/or his organization. Craig's surveillance team then watched the locations until the suspects' actions appeared illegal and/or gave them enough probable cause to react. If they (the surveillance team) witness a trunk-to-trunk, they get to choose how they want to steer or wrap up the case. Usually a handoff team might choose to first stop both vehicles and if it turns out the suspicious activity they witnessed was a narcotics transaction then with the seized narcotics they are able to obtain search warrants and go after the houses.

Observations by the surveillance team are what made the case. A Police surveillance team can follow anyone they want, but if that person is doing no wrong you have a group of highly paid individuals following Suzy Citizen to and from work or her children's afterschool activities. What I'm trying to say is by me giving a surveillance team starting information about a potential narcotics trafficker (Max) and that team is later able to make observations that lead to arrests and narcotics seizures it is then a confirmation that all of my other beliefs based on similar observations are also accurate. With that information in hand, a search warrant for locations connected to this organization but in another state is easily obtained.

With search warrant in hand, investigators enter the location and search for any evidence of the crime. Weapons, drugs and relating paraphernalia are looked for and seized. Paperwork, however, is the real target of any search warrant. Suspects paperwork such as pay-n-owe (who paid and who owes money) sheets, storage lockers receipts, bank account statements, mortgage account information can and often give a complete view of the criminal organization.

Money Laundering:

Narcotics and drug dealing are a cash business. In order to prevent drug dealers from having easy access to their *ill-gotten gains* – that phrase was actually in a couple of my money laundering manuals – banks, brokers, cash houses, automobile dealers, to name a few, are required to notify the IRS of large cash transactions (any cash transaction involving over $10,000). Legitimate transactions are no problem, however, if there are no viable explanations of where the money came from, the money can be seized through asset forfeiture.

A person is guilty of money laundering when they take money earned from illegal activities and attempt to make it appear as if earned by legal means. When a person is charged with money laundering, we are usually talking about extremely large sums of money, tens of thousands to millions or even billions of dollars.

Money laundering is big business, especially thanks to narcotics traffickers. I read an article that said narcotic trafficker's proceeds can exceed the weight of their initial product. Think about it, per the U.S. Department of the Treasury, one U.S. note weighs one gram and 454 notes equal one pound. So doing the math, $1,000,000 in five dollar bills would weigh a little more than 440 pounds; in ten's it would be just over 220 pounds; twenties would weigh about 110 pounds; fifties it would weigh out at 44 pounds and hundreds would be 22 pounds. Paying with cash is one way to hide illicit proceeds but lugging around suitcases of money to do so is simply not practical nor is it safe.

Are the profits that high? Look at it this way, wholesale cost for a kilo of cocaine is averaging right around $28,000. In Alaska and Hawaii, it's about $45,000 a kilo wholesale. The retail price of cocaine is about $100 a gram and there are 1,000 grams in a kilo gram. Again, doing the math, buying one kilo for $28,000 will net you a profit of about $170,000.

Nope my math's not off. I simply forgot to mention a common business practice of 'stepping on' – cutting the drug with an inert agent to increase the volume – thus doubling the amount of product being sold. Depending on where in the food chain the dealer is that purchases the cocaine, determines the purity and how many times he can 'step on it' to increase his profit without losing customers. Crack and Rock cocaine (which are highly addictive because they are the smoke-able versions of cocaine) are simply cocaine processed with baking soda.

Because of the high profit of drugs and the law created to prevent criminals from enjoying their illicit proceeds, an industry need was identified and several entrepreneurs scurried to fill the positions. Money launderers are business men and women who can easily move large sums of money without drawing much attention.

Examples of organizations money launderers use to 'clean' money: Restaurants, casinos, banks, cash houses, money exchanges, and jewelry stores to name a few. Most money launderers earn 5-10% of the total of the money they 'clean.'

Informants

There are two types of informants, Mercenary Informants and Citizen Informants.

Mercenary Informants: Expect something from their actions. A mercenary informant can be a person arrested with narcotics and given an option to help the police take down two or three other dealers for consideration in their own case. In other words, if they aid Law Enforcement with the arrest of other dealers at the same level or higher than them, in exchange the Deputy District Attorney (DDA) or Assistant United States Attorney (AUSA) will consider dropping or reducing criminal charges against them.

Another type of mercenary informant is a person who will infiltrate a criminal organization and give Law Enforcement information for a fee. Seriously, the money can be really good. Good informants can get a percentage of the seizure or a certain amount of money for each kilogram, pound or other unit of narcotic found.

Citizen Informant Usually a person who leaves an anonymous tip about suspicious activity.

Informants are classified as either Confidential Informants (CIs) or Confidential Reliable Informants (CRIs).

> A CI is simply an informant whose information has not yet been verified.
>
> A CRI is an informant that has recently proven his information is timely, accurate and solid.

That one letter – *R*, for reliable – can mean the difference between getting a search warrant or not. It's the job of the investigating officer to verify and validate their informant's story and information. Validation is extremely important, especially when getting to court. Judges are not too enamored with informants in the first place, it's a trust issue, so to have their information taken as fact they need to be proved Reliable with listed examples of how and when their information was proven accurate.

Citizen Informants are viewed as inherently trustworthy by various courts because they usually have nothing to gain from giving the information to Law Enforcement. In essence they come with a readymade CRI classification.

Either group of informants will have some type of history with the narcotic organization involved. A simple truth, good informants must be well versed in the drug culture, which changes daily, in order to be effective. This usually means the informant is in some way, shape or form connected to or affiliated with either members of a drug organization or is a dealer themselves.

Trust is in short supply when dealing with informants. Officers and agents have to be constantly reminded not to give up any information during the informant debriefing. If not careful when asking questions about what the informant knows, a new investigator can reveal a lot of what he knows about a particular organization.

Most narcotic units are housed in an off-site location from their Department/Agency in an attempt to keep their U/Cs out of the public eye. My Department had a policy not to bring informants into our office. First, we didn't want them to see and know all of our U/Cs. We never knew when we might be doing a case on a former snitch.

Next, we didn't want them to know where our CA-DOJ office was because they could attempt to stake it out to figure out our comings and goings. Not to mention target our U/C vehicles. All of our vehicles doubled as our office and home. I slept many a night in my car. Nearly every U/C unit has multiple weapons, surveillance gear & gadgets, case notes, target lists with addresses, not to mention personal equipment and toys.

Lastly, Investigative Units have wall charts, case files, information bulletins and other intelligence up on walls, lying on desks and written on white boards. The information, especially in a Task Force setting, usually covered a wide local, state and sometimes federal area. CI's business was the sale of information and there was no doubt in my mind – if we provided them with the opportunity – they would sell any information they could glean from us.

Policy dictated every time, at every meeting, there would be two officers meeting with the informant. If the CI was a female, every attempt was made to have a female present, even if the female was a non-sworn employee. We tried to have the same two officers driving the same vehicle meet with the CI every time. Am I giving you the impression cops really don't trust informants?

I've always believed the really good informants were the ones smart enough to feed police information about rivals and get Law Enforcement to take care of their competition. But as usual when dealing with rivals, the information obtained can be sketchy or dated.

> - Does your LEO work surveillance or U/C Operations, is s/he the U/C operative or are they one of the ones in charge? What is their goal and how will they set about accomplishing it?

Chapter Four

Homicide & Sex Crimes

<u>Homicide</u>

There are several incidents, some of which are not crimes, involving the death of an individual, and they are not equal. Each crime has its own specific element. Homicide is not synonymous with murder.

Murder is the unlawful killing of one person by another.

Homicide is the killing of one person by another and, as defined, is broader and includes:

- Justifiable (self-defense, military action during war or the use of deadly force by police officers)
- Manslaughter (without premeditation)
- Murder

Suicide, the killing of one's self, is not homicide. And neither is an unattended death which becomes simply a death investigation.

So all murders are homicides, but not all homicides are murder.

The job of a Homicide Detective is to figure out if the homicide they are investigating is Justifiable, Manslaughter or Murder. The Homicide Detective's starting point and where their investigation begins is an already established crime scene. Most homicide investigations begin with a call-out. I received a hat from a mid-western homicide detective, on the hat was his team's motto – Our day begins when yours ends – and their mascot a vulture.

Before a Homicide team ever reaches the scene, Patrol, who usually arrives first, seals the perceived crime scene and starts gathering witnesses. As soon as Patrol realizes it's an obvious homicide they call out their Patrol Supervisor who takes charge of the scene and makes sure protocol is followed until he (the Patrol Supervisor) relinquishes the scene to Homicide.

Something To Think About (STTA): Call out procedures for Homicide Teams differ from Agency to Agency. Each Department creates a call out policy depending on that which best suits their staffing, resources, needs of the community.

The Patrol Supervisor will have his officers gather and interview witnesses. He will prepare a briefing sheet that contains:

- How patrol was notified of the homicide (was it a stabbing where the person died, did they get a call of shots fired and locate a body, was an abandoned car being towed and the tow operator smelled death)?
- Who found the body and what position was it in on arrival?
- What witnesses are or were present at the time of death?
- Who pronounced death and when?
- How and when was the scene was sealed.

Once the Patrol Supervisor briefs the entire homicide team, the scene and the case are no longer considered the responsibility of patrol, it is now Homicide's show.

As the on-scene Homicide Supervisor is briefed, with his team, he decides who is going to do what and where the case is going to land. Usually the case is assigned to the person with the smallest amount of open cases. If the homicide seems complex or high profile the supervisor will usually call upon his go-to investigator (that person, with experience, who knows how to get the job done).

Below are the steps and method of investigating a scene.

Arrival at the Scene: Investigators must always assume the criminal has left physical evidence. If there are any victims remaining at the scene who are still breathing first priority is to provide medical assistance (yes, you do have to tell some rookies to do this – it's better if you wait until they finish being ill) and guide Emergency Medical Services (EMS) through the scene if necessary.

Something To Think About (STTA): If an officer rolls (arrives) onto a scene and sees a person laying face down it is the officer's responsibility to determine if that person is breathing or has a pulse. If the person is not obviously dead (decapitated, in beginning stages of rigor mortis, decomposing) the officer is required to perform CPR until Paramedics arrive. Paramedics can pronounce death if they are supervised by a Medical Doctor usually via radio or phone. LEOs (Law Enforcement Officers) are highly discouraged from pronouncing death.

In Fact, many Agencies have policies in place reminding their officers they are not medical professionals and are therefore not to pronounce death. They add to that, any officer who fails to perform CPR or other life saving medical assistance, is considered guilty of pronouncing death. Good way to get in a butt load of trouble.

The Crime Scene: The crime scene includes the immediate area where the crime occurred as well as:

- The entry route
- Escape route
- Vehicles
- Secondary locations (waiting spots, hiding places and all avenues to and from those locations)

Protect the scene and its contents – This is usually difficult because numerous people have walked around and through the crime scene. It's bad enough to have civilian lookie-loos, but any officer close enough will swing by. All extraneous foot traffic can muck up a crime scene. Patrol or the first Law Enforcement Officer (LEO) on scene should have blocked off and sealed the scene. You as the investigator simply don't know how much of your scene is contaminated.

Process the Scene – It's important to inspect the scene from all sides and angles. It's said every crime scene has a story to tell and the Crime Scene Investigator needs to listen to and read that story. Once the scene is sketched and photographed, Forensics are allowed to process the evidence at the scene.

I was asked, *several times,* to mention that Forensic Technicians DO NOT investigate nor do they solve crimes. Their job is to collect, preserve and interpret evidence. One Investigator asked me to say if you see one (Forensic Technician) wearing a gun – run. I've never watched a full episode of Crime Scene Investigations (CSI) but I know this is a touchy subject with Homicide Detectives.

Objectives while at the Scene:
  • Reconstruct the incident

- Identify the sequence of events
- Determine the method of operation
- Find a motive for the crime
- Identify what was taken
- Determine EVERYTHING the criminal may have done
- Recover ALL evidence that will aid the investigation

Either as the scene is processed or when it's done being processed, the body is ready to be moved. Enter the Coroner. The Coroner is the one who investigates the body. He/she will move the body, check the contents of the clothing and begin their physical exam there at the scene. The one test I always remember is the taking of the liver temperature.

While at the scene of a fatal traffic collision (T/C), I pointed out to my trainee that the Deputy Coroner was about to take the liver temperature. My trainee walked over to watch what the Deputy was doing, the Deputy offered my trainee the thermometer and asked if she would like to take a stab at getting the temperature. Then he (the Deputy Coroner) laughed hysterically at his own joke. My trainee took a step back and gave me a concerned glance then rested her hand on her gunbelt near her weapon. I simply laughed and shrugged. What could I say, most Coroners are a bit strange.

Something To Think About (STTA): Eighty-five percent of the population secretes their blood type from other body fluids such as sweat, saliva, semen and urine. It's possible to collect DNA classification from some of those samples.

Best way to collect biological evidence is to let it air dry and put it in a paper bag. Plastic bags, containers, glass jars or other nonporous packaging can aid bacteria growth that can damage the sample.

Today all states have a guideline on which convicted offenders must provide DNA samples to be entered into the FBI CODIS (Combined DNA Index System) Database. Some states require all convicted felons to supply DNA evidence, this is making it much easier to identify perpetrators by their DNA.

Locate, Identify and Sequester Witnesses: This includes canvassing the area and going door to door, as well as checking for relevant vehicles, weapons, physical evidence etc. Again, if patrol did their job, Homicide should have groups of witnesses to re-interview. The key word here is RE-interview. Patrol's initial interview of potential witnesses is extremely important. During the initial interview, the witness can be locked into a story. This is important because later the witnesses' account of events can be tainted by speculation, other witness accounts or strong emotions.

Once the victim is identified and suspects determined, let the interviews begin. In the next chapter I will get into interviews and interrogations.

The more serious crime is the one given precedent – usually homicide trumps everything else. If drugs are found at the scene, Homicide will usually call in a member of Narcotics for Intelligence. Homicide is still in the driver's seat and calling the shots. The same is true with gang related homicides.

Sex Crimes

Sex crimes are investigated in much the same way as a homicide. If possible, the scene is sealed and every bit of evidence is logged and recorded. Next the victim needs to be examined for physical evidence. A lot of jurisdictions have SART (Sexual Assault Response Teams). SART is a combination of Law Enforcement, SAFE (Sexual Assault Forensic Examiners – usually RNs), Rape Crisis Advocates, and Prosecutors. The RNs are sometimes referred to as Forensic Nurses. SART RNs are trained in collecting, documenting and preserving evidence from any sexual assault or rape case.

Rape: A major difference between a Homicide Investigation and a Sexual Assault Crime (when the victim lives) is collection of evidence. At a Homicide Investigation, the body is usually the last thing examined. For a sexual assault the opposite is true, it's imperative to get the victim to medical treatment as soon as possible. To further complicate matters the victim should not be allowed to change clothes, bathe, drink water or otherwise use the bathroom without permission from medical personnel.

Because rape is so traumatic, another purpose of SART is to help the victim through their ordeal, both physically and emotionally, while doing what is necessary to convict the rapist and protect the community. The primary focus of SART is the victim, with conviction being a strong secondary goal.

Child Pornography: Illegal pictorial materials involving children. Research shows most child pornography is created by people with access to children: Family members, family friends, babysitters, coaches. The National Center for Missing and Exploited Children (NCMEC) (http://www.missingkids.com) is a great resource. They have publications and manuals covering everything you might want to know and even more that you might pay to *never* learn about.

During my stint with Sexual Predators Apprehension Task Force (SPAT), I used NCMEC to help me identify victims in the materials I had seized. NCMEC has a database of photos and acts as a clearinghouse. They put me in contact with the Agency that held the information needed for my case.

Possession of Child Pornography is bad, but the sentencing for that crime is mild. Manufacturing or distributing Child Porn carries severe sentences. To get a conviction for manufacturing or distributing child porn, investigators must identify the victim. In this arena National Center for Missing and Exploited Children is a great clearing house as well as resource for Law Enforcement.

Something To Think About (STTA): A recently released, twice convicted, sex offender moved in across the street from Megan Kanka in 1994. No one in the neighborhood knew of Jesse Timmendequas' background. Megan's Law was a result of the rape and murder of seven year old Megan. In 1996, Federal Megan's Law was passed and now all states have a sex offender database that identifies convicted sex offenders living in every neighborhood.

The following FBI website provides links to every states Megan's Law website.
(http://www.fbi.gov/scams-safety/registry/registry)

Traveler Cases: A lot of sexual predators do not like to hunt for victims in their own backyard. One method of locating and identifying a target is over the internet. 'Travelers' are predators who target children in other states or cities. The predator sets out to become the child's friend and works hard to develop a bond based on secrets. The predator may start by sending the victim pornography and encouraging him/her to reciprocate with the goal of getting the victim to send self created pornographic photos.

Each time the victim complies with their friend's demands, the predator sends them a gift. The greater the demand the better the gift. This continues until the predator convinces the victim to meet. A sexual predator will travel great distances for a 'willing' victim.

Today, social networks are more popular than ever and children at younger and younger ages are accessing the internet. Bottom line, with the internet and all of the social media outlets, sexual predators have never had a better forum for access to our children.

How wired is too wired?

November 2010, Rachel Ann Hicks, thirty-six year old, mother of two, met a 13 year old boy in an x-box chat room. After exchanging illicit photos with the juvenile who she told she was twenty-three, Hicks flew to Maryland over Thanksgiving. Hicks raped the boy.

- So, do you know what your child is doing on-line? Are you sure?

Chapter Five

Interviewing vs. Interrogation

Recently I had a lively discussion with a few of my Law Enforcement buddies regarding Interviewing vs. Interrogation. My contention was interviewing had more to do with getting information in a friendly manner where interrogation was completely and totally adversarial. I was told, in no uncertain terms, I was Bug Nuts (trust me they didn't say it that nicely).

A friend of mine, TD, told me every interrogation starts as an interview. I agreed with that, but I added the caveat that even after the Miranda warning has been read and waived, the best information gathering happened when the 'interrogation' remained an interview. To this we were in complete agreement.

To say my views of interviewing and interrogation have dramatically changed since my Academy Training is an understatement. I will go into that a little later in this chapter.

First, I will explain Miranda and give you some updates then, I will go into Interview vs. Interrogation.

<u>Miranda</u>

"You have the right to remain silent.

Anything you say can and will be used against
  you in a court of law.

You have the right to an attorney.

If you cannot afford an attorney, one will be
  provided for you.

Do you understand the rights I have just read
  to you?

With these rights in mind, do you wish to
  speak to me?"

Anybody who's ever seen a cop show knows, probably by heart, the above Miranda Advisement. Trouble is, many don't understand, especially Hollywood, the mechanics behind the law.

The easiest way to remember Miranda is: Custody + Questioning = Miranda Warning. That's how I remembered the reasons and need for Miranda. The person must be in custody and I had to be questioning them regarding the case in order for Miranda to apply.

Hollywood has made a ton of money perpetuating the false belief that anyone not advised of their Miranda Rights is subject to immediate release for all charges brought against them. The purpose of Miranda is to make sure a person understands their rights under the 5th and 6th Amendments to the U.S. Constitution.

Miranda is not, nor has it ever been, a get out of jail free card.

Failure to advise a subject of Miranda after he has been arrested will simply result in the suppression of any information gathered during that specific questioning.

For example, a woman is arrested for beating and kicking her husband to death. All the way to jail the officer questions her about why she did it. She tells the officer she didn't mean to kill her husband but she was tired of asking him to put the toilet seat down. She lost her temper and when she came to her senses her husband was lying on the floor in a pool of blood.

At the scene her blood soaked clothes were seized. Photographs of her raw, bruised and bloody hands were taken. Her shoes that had tufts of the victim's hair and clothing fibers were also confiscated. After completing the booking process, the officer goes to question the suspect. The officer fails to read her Miranda rights and just continues the friendly dialogue started on the drive to jail.

Question: Is she going to be released from jail? Will all the charges be dropped?

Answer: Heck no. Just like the original case, Miranda v Arizona 1966, all statements and confessions are inadmissible in court if the person is not advised of his rights. Miranda was retried without the confession and he was convicted based on evidence obtained independent of the confession. The same would be the case for the woman in the hypothetical case above.

There are questions the suspect is required to answer with or without Miranda. Questions that identify who he is, medical issues, and any other questions pertaining to the booking process must be answered. Requirements to answer and provide driver's license, registration and insurance information comes from authority given or rather signed away when a person signs for (accepts) their driver's license.

Miranda only covers protecting the subject from answering questions regarding the crime for which they have been arrested. It protects their 5th Amendment Rights regarding Self-incrimination.

Officers can use the questions asked prior to arrest. Remember custody. The person must be under arrest or not otherwise allowed to leave. During the investigative (information gathering) portion of the contact, the suspect can come and go as they please. This means they are not in custody. So as long as you are not solely basing whether you arrest on his answer, it is fair to use his answers without advising Miranda.

An officer can also use information a suspect blabbers on about as long as the officer does not ask any questions. Of course, it's best to try to stop the suspect from talking or if he continues on to stop him and then read him his Miranda Rights. If he waives them, fine, let him go on chatting and finish the interview at the jail. If he decides to invoke his rights – fine. In any event, officers can still use the unsolicited statements.

You arrest a subject for hit-and-run driving. After transporting to jail and booking, you take the subject to interview room and read him his Miranda rights. You ask him if he understands the rights as you've read them to him. He answers yes. Then you ask him if he want to answer some questions and he does not answer. You begin to question him. He confesses to the crime. Can you use his statements against him?

A fairly recent development on Miranda happened June 1st 2010, the Supreme Court decided (http://www.supremecourt.gov/opinions/09pdf/08-1470.pdf) if a person fails to invoke their Miranda Right and later answers questions it is perfectly correct to assume their answering a question is waiving their Miranda Rights. Previously, it was presumed that a person's failure to answer the question portion of Miranda was their invocation of their rights.

Interviewing v. Interrogation

When I went through the California Highway Patrol (CHP) Academy we spent ten hours on interrogation techniques. Most of those hours were spent reviewing the 1966 Supreme Court ruling on Miranda v. Arizona where the Miranda Warning originated. At the end of our class, we were given a practical exam were the cadets questioned each other.

To say I learned little about Interview and Interrogation techniques is an understatement. When I hit the field my first training officer taught me to take my cues about what happened from the physical evidence all around me. As a CHP Officer, my primary duties were traffic so that meant lots of accident reports.

I was taught to have a pretty good idea of how the accident happened before I ever talked to either party involved. I let physical evidence be the guide by which I decided if the person being interviewed was being truthful. My mind was pretty much made up before I spoke to anyone. Believe it or not, this approach aided me with learning some basic avoidance mannerisms.

By watching how the parties to the accident answered my questions – direct eye contact or stare at their feet, gesture wildly or give answers that seemed like questions – I was able to learn and recognize deceptive behavior. Every person I spoke with helped me sharpen my interviewing skills. Based on their responses to my questions, I learned how to zero in on the questions they didn't want asked.

One of my training officers attempted to teach me how to interview. At the time I didn't understand what he did, much less how he did it. The driver of a hit and run vehicle had turned himself in at one of the local police stations. Because I was investigating the accident I was dispatched to the Covina Police Department. The suspect and his sister were waiting for me in the lobby. Covina PD allowed my training officer and me to use one of their interrogation rooms for our interview.

In the interrogation room was a table with three chairs, two of which were on one side of the table. I moved to sit on the side of the table with two chairs so the suspect could sit across from me and my Field Training Officer (FTO). My FTO maneuvered me into the one seat and sat across the table from me next to the suspect. I thought it was weird, but hey, he was in charge.

I introduced myself and asked the suspect his name and additional identifying information. After writing down everything he provided, I explained why we were there and told him I needed to read him his Miranda Rights. Technically I didn't need to, but on our drive to Covina my FTO (Don) had told me to, so I did.

Using a CHP card, I read the suspect his Miranda Rights. When I began to read the Miranda Advisement questions from the card Don interrupted and offered the suspect a smoke. The man said yes, accepted the cigarette and both the suspect and Don lit up. Once they were both relaxed and puffing away I started, once again, to ask the Miranda Advisement questions.

Don interrupted me. Again. But this time he followed the interruption with one of his patented 'you're pissing me off, Taylor' looks. So, I put my Miranda Card down and said nothing else. Don talked to the suspect about cigarettes, cars, girls, everything under the sun except the car accident. They chatted about nothing for fifteen minutes or more. Eventually, Don asked and received a waiver of all the suspect's rights, but he phrased it a lot differently than was on my CHP Miranda Card.

Don proceeded to get a full confession of all the elements of hit and run. I watched my FTO become the suspect's friend and then get him to tell his new best buddy everything. I saw it, but had no clue how to duplicate it. When we arrived at our unit after the interview, I told Don there was no way was I smoking just to get a confession. Don suggested I buy a pack of cigarettes to share.

Cigarettes were the least of my worries. My FTO explained how becoming friends or being friendly with the suspect would yield more information than adversarial contact. I'm not sure what my issue was, but at that time I just couldn't grasp the concept.

Based on that interview, the Deputy District Attorney filed charges of hit and run against the man Don interviewed. Of course, I wrote all the reports.

When I left the CHP and went to the California Department of Justice, Bureau of Narcotic Enforcement (BNE), I worked narcotics for ten years. My marginal interviewing skills dropped dramatically and I simply interrogated everyone. When my team took down dope dealers we usually ended up with narcotics in hand. My interrogation went something like:

"Who'd you get the dope from?"

"We caught you with fifty kilograms of cocaine in your possession, you can either work for us or go to jail."

"If you give me your supplier, I'll tell the District Attorney you cooperated. That can go a long way to helping you."

If they pleaded innocence or victim of circumstance, I walked out the door and didn't look back. Most times, the suspects would tell us of storage lockers, additional locations and dealers we may have missed. A lot of times suspects knew they had to make a deal fast or someone else, usually arrested with them, would.

During my time with BNE, I did hone my skills as an undercover (U/C) officer and learned how to role play in order to buy dope. I took several courses on Interviewing and Interrogation, but not for follow up information once the case was taken down. I took those classes in order to obtain the information I needed to be more effective as an U/C agent. I never had much trouble getting people to talk, those classes helped me to get suspects to talk about topics important to me.

When I left Narcotics for the Division of Gaming Control (DGC) I quickly realized I was in sore need of better interviewing skills. On my first fraud case, thank goodness I took a partner with me for the interview. I nearly blew the case I was working against a customer who frequented one of the Southern California card clubs. I gathered all the information, prepped my case and was ready for the interview.

My partner for this case was Dave, a veteran Special Agent who had worked investigations for years. Dave was only along for the ride, it was my case and I was to be handling everything. When we sat down in the suspect's home to begin the interrogation, I realized I had nothing to force the subject's compliance. I was there to get a confession and without the suspect's admittance of the elements of the crime, I was dead in the water. I think I opened and closed my mouth several times like a fish out of water. Dave read my body language – but really how hard could it have been with me looking blank, glossy eyed and confused – and took over the interview.

It was like watching Don all over again. But this time I was able to call upon my role playing experiences as a U/C making friends as I attempted to pull together all the elements of the crimes committed. I watched Dave befriend the suspect by chatting about the nice neighborhood and his house and furnishings. Dave was able to get the information I was seeking, but I walked away with so much more that night.

While with DGC, I began to hone my interviewing skills. I learned how to befriend and chat before I began my interview. I took more classes on interviewing and completely stopped thinking or using the word interrogation when I sat down with suspects.

After Gaming, I went to CA-DOJ's California Bureau of Investigation (CBI), Sexual Predator Apprehension Team (SPAT). Here everything came together for me as far as my interviewing skills. My job encompassed investigation of registered sex offenders (anyone convicted of certain sex crimes is required by law to register with their local Law Enforcement Agency), child pornography, child molestation, traveler cases, serial rapists, child abductions and any other cases for which a local Agency requests assistance.

For registered sex offender sweeps, our team would hit an area and knock on doors to make sure registered sex offenders were living where they reported they were. We also questioned neighbors to make sure the offender was in compliance with the registration laws. If the suspect was on parole, we would contact his/her parole officer and request permission to search his home.

> **Something To Think About (STTA):** Parolees have 4th Amendment Waivers which means their Parole Officer or an agent for their Parole Officer can search their residence at any time without a search warrant. Something many people don't think about, if a parent allows a child who is a parolee to live in their home with them, that home would then be susceptible to the 4th Amendment Waiver.

On a particular sweep we were working with California Parole so we planned on making quite a few searches of the premises. During one of those sweeps we contacted a homeowner who had a registered sex offender as a roommate. The homeowner told us the registered sex offender only stayed at the house a few days during the week – violation of the offender's parole. Any sex offender who consistently spends one or more nights away from his primary residence is considered to have a secondary residence. There is no problem with a sex offender having multiple homes as long as each residence is disclosed on his registration form. In this case the sex offender failed to mention any other residence.

We then started searching the area of the house that was the Parolee's domain. The owner of the residence followed me around the house talking to me. I remained friendly but some of the statements he made started to send up red flags. I sat down and began to talk with the owner in earnest. We chatted about how put upon he was and how his friends and roommates took complete advantage of him.

He told me how some of his friends would drop off small children and leave them in his care. My supervisor gave me the cut signal, but there was more here. I broke off my conversation, went to my supervisor and told him—based on the man's freely given statements to me—I believed the homeowner was molesting children. He told me to get as much information as I could.

Being given a green light, I became the homeowner's new best friend. I secured his permission to search his living space and I obtained his waiver to Miranda. Although it took some time, I also obtained a confession that he had molested two of his 'friends' children. I commiserated with him, I agreed that a three year old could be sexually provocative and it was hard for a man to say no when enticed so strongly. Most importantly, I was able to convince him I meant it.

During all of our conversations I did not judge him, belittle or embarrass him. I received enough information to follow-up on the identity of the children and prepared a case file for the district attorney to file molestation charges.

Every time I saw him in court I was friendly. Never did I switch to adversarial in dealing with him. I wanted to. I didn't bitch slap him because of his belief a three-year-old could be a vixen. I wanted to. I remained his friend through conviction when he was remanded to the custody of the court. I didn't laugh and say good as the bailiff walked him back to the holding cell. I so wanted to.

But more than these wants, I needed the next cop's job to be as easy as possible in having this scum self-incriminate himself. Because sooner than later, he would get out. Regardless of what I wanted.

So which is better, interviewing or interrogation? At the beginning of my career I would have said interrogation. Toward the end, I would have said Interviewing. It's funny, now that I look back, I realize it's all about personal preference. Some LEO's are good at getting information through adversarial contact with their suspect. Others get information by building relationships. Suspects, too, will be more receptive to one type of interviewer over the other.

- So which system works best? What type of cop is your LEO? Which situation would he be more comfortable in? There's your answer.

Chapter Six

Networking: A Cop's & Your Character's Greatest Investigative Tool

When I left the California Highway Patrol (CHP) and hired on with the California Department of Justice, Bureau of Narcotic Enforcement (BNE), my first assignment was the Inland Empire Clandestine Laboratory Task Force (IECLTF). IECLTF was a true Task Force consisting of all the major Agencies (City, County and Federal) in the region.

I was dropped into the middle of a surveillance team, handed car keys to a huge and really ugly POS car, a pager and state credit cards, and was told to keep up, pay attention and learn. My two CA-DOJ Academy classmates who reported to Riverside BNE with me were a lot more familiar with narcotics than I was. Pete had worked for IECLTF as a Riverside County Deputy Sheriff, so he already knew everyone in the Task Force. Roy came from a Los Angeles County Police Department and had work narcotics alongside a different BNE Task Force.

The CHP had a manual and a policy for just about every contingency. When I arrived at my CHP office I was told what was expected of me and immediately assigned a Field Training Officer (FTO). From the CA-DOJ Academy I could tell BNE was a lot less structured than I was used to. At the Academy, as Special Agent Trainees, if you will were housed in a hotel (with maid service) and given food allowance and a membership to a gym so we could exercise. Sometime I'll have to tell you about my CHP Academy time.

When I hit the field, my first day on surveillance for BNE lasted four – I reported to work Monday morning and didn't make it back home until Thursday night. We spent those days following around a hyped up Clandestine Laboratory (Clan Lab) cooker (person who manufactures meth) as he bought supplies. Nothing says welcome to narcotics like three and a half days of living in your car.

During that investigation we identified, located and took down a 'bubbling lab' (a meth lab that is actively in the process of manufacturing methamphetamine). I could only do grunt work because I was not yet Clandestine laboratory Safety Certified. After all the crooks were in jail and the lab site processed (evidence gathered and the remaining contaminated material properly disposed and all evidence processed) we were told the next day we would have a mandatory team meeting at the office.

Just prior to the team meeting we three newbies were brought into the Supervisors office and given our expectations to pass probation: For our first assignment, generate a lead for a case and perform in the capacity as a Case Agent. We were given thirty days to accomplish our task. Each of us were then assigned FTO's who would both assist us and supervise our progress. Both Pete and Roy's FTO's walked into the office when called, I was told my FTO was on vacation and wouldn't be in the office for another week.

During the team meeting the three of us were introduced as the new Special Agents, like they hadn't seen us the last four days out on surveillance. It was obvious, through the banter, Pete and Roy already had a connection with many of the people in the room, especially their FTO's. After the introductions, the Supervisor opened the floor for case updates and pitching. Everyone present talked about how and why their case should be the next one worked.

Both Pete and Roy pitched a case to be worked. I could understand Pete having a case, he had worked the area. He knew everyone and was on home turf. But Roy and I both came from out of the area Police Agencies. When questioned about the case Roy presented, he said he had contacted one of his old team members and they passed on information that one of their targets moved into our area. As a favor to

Roy, his PD buddy turned over that portion of the case to him.

Well hell, looked like I was the only person out in the cold as far as cases were concerned, and the clock was ticking. I started trying to generate a case by reviewing and doing follow-up on We-Tips and Precursor Reports submitted to our department.

Something To Think About (STTA): We-Tip is a national organization that encourages people to give information about crime in their area. The information can be anonymous (majority) or with follow-up information (extremely rare). The crime tips for the area are batched together and shipped to any Agency that will follow-up on them.

Methamphetamine is manufactured. Most of the chemicals needed to manufacture meth are regulated and referred to as Precursors. Monthly Precursor reports are generated regarding the sales and distribution of those chemicals used to manufacture methamphetamine. Any spike of sales for any of the needed chemicals would be a great starting point for a potential Clan Lab case.

When not out on surveillance, I was pouring over We-Tips and Precursor reports. I generated several leads, but every time I presented my potential case it was shot down in favor of more timely (a lot of the information I referenced was at least thirty days old) and reliable information. I was told if I could compile information about massive amounts of chemicals being sold, that would garner me a chance at getting a case. I was trying hard to get a case generated before my FTO arrived at the office.

The day I was introduced to Jerry, my FTO, I found out why I was the one selected to wait for an FTO. Apparently, Jerry was the only officially trained FTO in Riverside. Everyone felt I was the only person, out of the three who arrived, that really needed to be trained. I chose to ignore the insult, even though wrong on so many levels. Instead, I choose to see the whole situation as a positive. After all, out of the three of us, I was going to be the only one who was trained by a POST (Peace Officers Standards and Training) certified and CA-DOJ selected Trainer. That meant, I didn't have to wade through misinformation or bad habits. Yep, on this one, I was definitely being given the advantage.

Jerry informed me my supervisors were concerned I had yet to submit a case. When I thought of the number of We-Tips I followed up on and Precursor Reports I reviewed, I started to get angry. Jerry understood why I hadn't generated a viable case. He explained he was as new to Riverside BNE and working Meth as I was and would do no better generating a Clan Lab case.

Wasn't that just ducky? Not only did I have a week delay getting my FTO, but said FTO was useless when it came to lab cases. His forte was cocaine cases.

About this time, I began to wonder if I was being set up for failure and I asked Jerry as much. Of course, he said no, they wanted me to succeed which is why I was assigned to him – (I did tell you all cops had major egos, right?) My FTO knew how to work major cocaine cases and believed if you knew how to work a basic investigation you could work any investigation. At this time, he introduced me to all the information and search systems available to Law Enforcement and he taught me how to access them and the way to optimize the results of any search.

Jerry was determined to have my stats exceed both Pete and Roy's numbers combined. (Why did I always receive FTO's who were overachievers?) His contention: Investigative skills would trump home field advantages and a week's head start. After a few calls, we developed information on a gang banger with an outstanding arrest warrant indicating he was also a Phencyclidine (PCP) Manufacturer in a small city in the Inland Empire.

My FTO and I drove to the residence city of our PCP manufacturer. On the way, Jerry briefed me on the reputation of the Police Department in the city. The department was supposedly known for screwing over other Agencies. It was said that PD would use any information shared to increase the department's arrest statistics.

Jerry liked to make his own mind up about incidents based on first hand information rather than hearsay and conjecture. He added the most effective LEOs (Law Enforcement Officers) were those who effectively developed connections with a variety of officers and departments. It was harder to screw someone over if you knew them or met them face to face. My FTO believed personality conflicts were at the base of most issues.

When we arrived at the Police Department, we went to the Watch Commander's office and Sergeant (Sgt.) Richard listened as I laid out my entire case and requested any information on contacts between the suspect and the police department that could help me develop enough probable cause to gain a search warrant. Sgt Richard didn't seem to want to be bothered with us and told us to contact the detective's bureau for the information we needed. He was a bit abrupt and not a little rude. As we walked out of his office the Sgt asked when we would be serving the warrant. Jerry remained friendly and said I was still writing it (the search warrant) so not before Thursday.

In the Detectives bullpen I went over my case again. The detectives were a little friendlier than Sgt Richard and I do mean a very little. One outright interrogated me for my information. I was about to tell him to go fornicate himself, when Jerry put his hand on my shoulder and took over the answering of the questions. Jerry talked and smoozed and reminded the detectives their Sgt sent us to them. Reluctantly we were given the information we sought and left.

As we drove to the residence of the suspect, to do an assessment of the location for the search warrant service, Jerry said he'd heard that police department also had an issue with women police officers, but didn't tell me because he didn't want me to go in with an attitude. I told him I was new to CA-DOJ, not to being a cop. I was used to AdamHenry's (A**h*les) on the job, but I was no one's butt boy or punching bag.

Jerry told me I did great, in fact he laughed. I effectively showed I wasn't a pushover and I didn't back down or roll over and give them everything they wanted. He said no amount of information, connection or case was worth putting up with abuse. So I asked why we didn't just leave and finish getting the case information elsewhere. It was then my FTO told me because he too was new to the area he was also trying to develop local connections.

Yes, maybe that PD was not a place where I could develop a strong network of officers, but he hoped he could. Which was why he took over the conversation, he then asked/stated if I noticed how he obtained the information we needed? I said yes, after he invoked their Sgt's name. He laughed again and shrugged his shoulders, simply reminding me he had obtained the information.

After I studied the suspect's home and made an assessment of the best way to enter the location, I made note of any area that could prove to be a trouble spot. I then took surveillance photos and noted all vehicles at the location. All day Tuesday was spent reviewing and compiling my intelligence and writing the search warrant.

I also had to prepare a briefing for my team which included everything from where the nearest hospital was to who was giving Knock/Notice and the order of people through the door. The best part about being Case Agent on a search warrant, according to Jerry, was putting yourself as the first person through the door. Because this was my first warrant I was instructed to give Knock/Notice and put my Academy mates on the entry team as well.

Something To Think About (STTA): Tactics on hitting a door during the service of the search warrant is pretty straight forward. Once the team is set at the door and ready to proceed, everyone is lined up along one side of the door and one officer with a battering ram (AKA Key to the City) is situated on the opposite side. The first person in line gives Knock/Notice. They bang on the door and yell, "Peace Officers. Search Warrant. Demand Entry."

The law requires officers wait a reasonable time for someone to come to the door, exception is if officers at the front door hear people running away from the front door or hear or can articulate a need to prevent the suspects from destroying evidence. If no one opens the door the officer standing on the opposite side of the door from the officer giving knock/notice can force entry – polite way of saying break down the door.

Once I finished all my paperwork, we headed to the court on Wednesday to get a Judge's signature. We were sent to a Judge's Chambers where the duty Judge read and reviewed my search warrant to make sure it had sufficient probable cause for issuance. Once the Judge was satisfied he signed my warrant making it valid and serviceable.

My search warrant briefing was scheduled for 0700 Thursday, (Search Warrants can only be served between 7AM and 10PM unless an exception is granted by a judge), with the search warrant service to immediately follow. Jerry was to call that local PD and get permission to use their parking lot as a staging area for the briefing and as a jump off point for the drive to the search warrant location.

I was pretty proud of my achievement and ready to get a search warrant under my belt. Jerry thundered over to my desk, told me to grab my stuff – we needed to roll. I wasn't sure why he was so pissed or where we were headed, but I was done with everything I had to do until the next morning so followed him out the door without argument.

My FTO's undercover (U/C) car was a newer Ford Mustang. He peeled out as we headed really fast to our unknown, at least to me, destination. We made it to the Police Department quite quickly in silence. I followed Jerry's determined stride past the dark and closed Watch Commander's door and into the empty detective's bullpen. I began to get a niggle we were being avoided.

Jerry left the bullpen, headed back to the front desk. He stopped at a clerk's desk and requested the Watch Commander. Funny, we'd just missed him. Same with the detectives. My FTO asked—control tight in each word—who he could talk to regarding *last night's* arrest of ***our*** suspect.

Yep, we were being avoided.

Turned out the arresting officer had just returned from court and the clerk—happy to turn us over to someone else—called him to the front desk to deal with us.

Jerry started with the fact he was told by Detective Butthead that he (the Patrol Officer) had arrested Joe Crook last night during a routine patrol stop. The Patrol Officer said Sgt. Dick (I mean Richard) briefed his shift last night before he went out and told him to look for Joe Crook—that along with outstanding warrants, the man was manufacturing PCP in their city. Sgt Dick had instructed the shift to find a way to get into the house any way possible.

The Patrol Officer had chased Joe Crook through his residence, (exigent circumstances and hot pursuit allow an officer either in an emergency or while chasing someone to follow legally follow them into a residence without a search warrant) but said he hadn't seen anything out of the ordinary. At that point, Jerry simply confirmed that the Sgt., he and I spoke to on Monday was the one who ordered Patrol to arrest my suspect. Once back in the car, Jerry apologized. He said what the Police Department had done was one of the worst forms of betrayal. There was no reason or excuse for their behavior, the hunt for statistics should never, ever supersede doing what was right.

Jerry was obviously upset, but I was pretty angry, too. I had done a lot of work I now had to undo. Not to mention how hyped up I'd been about serving the search warrant.

Back at the office, Jerry and I were immediately called into our supervisors' office to report. The first words out of my supervisor's mouth were that was not the norm. In fact, the more they spoke of it the angrier they became. It was funny and gratifying to see how angry everyone became at the actions of that police agency. The conversation in the supervisors' office went into the importance of establishing and preserving contacts, that a large majority of narcotic cases were made by one officer passing along a piece of information to a buddy or other Law Enforcement contact.

Betraying another Agency for a stat is considered a major, bozo no-no.

In the past, Jerry had taken down an organization with over seven million dollars in cash and hundreds of kilograms of cocaine. The way he developed the probable cause needed for his case was by:

- Passing off smaller portions of the case to local Agencies.
- He selected an Agency, calling someone he knew and offering them the case.
- If need be, depending on the importance of the case, he would cold call the nearest local Agency and attempt to establish a new contact.

- If unwilling to make the drive, he would he would call upon another out of area Agency to take the case.

- The more he trusted the Agency, the larger and more important the case Jerry would pass off to them.

- Case pipelines worked both ways.

- He said there would be times when his cases would dry up or trickle to a near stop and he would receive a call from one of his contacts passing off a case.

- Making a contact was important, but follow-up and follow through was what cemented the connection and made for longtime mutually benefiting partnerships and friendships.

Jerry stood by what he said about passing off cases—the back and forth part—that was how it was supposed to work. He wanted to make sure I wouldn't blow off networking because of this one bad experience. I eased his mind, promising I would only blow off that Agency. I would give everyone else at least one chance.

Both Jerry and I were transferred to INCA (INland Crackdown Allied Task Force) when it was created. Although no longer my FTO, Jerry and I worked together a lot. INCA was viewed as one of the top producing Crackdown teams in the state. We even received the Attorney General's Award for Excellence. On the road to that award we seized multiple tons of cocaine, several pounds of tar heroin, hundreds of pounds of methamphetamine and multiple tons of marijuana. Within one six month period, our team seized three different two ton loads and one three ton seizure of cocaine. We had also seized over six million dollars of drug money during that same time span.

Not once during my time with INCA did we call on that nameless police department for assistance or to give a handoff to them.

After four years on INCA, I was sent to HIDTA, Group 50 (High Intensity Drug Trafficking Area). When my team went up on wiretaps I was usually one of the Case Agents and, for the most part, one of the permanent wire room managers. One of my many jobs was to locate and call out 'handoff teams' (teams that would be given specific targets from the organization to work). I received a call from that police department that didn't like women and had screwed Jerry and me and was asked if I would consider making them a handoff team. I asked for the name of the Sgt in charge and was told it was Sgt Dick. So I said no. I told the person I couldn't trust his Sgt. or their investigations bureau when I had a small case. What made them think I would trust them now, with a larger one? Before I hung up, I told the person I was talking to to make sure they told their sergeant that Special Agent Margaret Taylor sent her regards.

It really felt good doing that.

I believe the world is a much smaller place than it seems. A lot of the connections I made while working Law Enforcement still stand. In fact, I still contact many of my old buddies for updates or clarifications to questions poised to me. I enjoy learning and sharing my knowledge.

Every one of your cop characters have a history and more than likely have made contacts far and wide. Agencies oft times need assistance and the detective or patrol person who answers the phone and gives the assistance has just made a friend and earned themselves a return favor. Your character may never call in that favor, but it doesn't negate the fact that someone in an Agency somewhere thinks well of your character and may pass their name along when one of their co-workers needs some help.

My point is that professional courtesy goes a long way and can help create lasting connections that can come in handy when you need them most. I will admit networking has always been my forte. But I don't know one successful cop that doesn't have a list of people he/she can call for a hand. And if I don't know someone then I ask one of my officer buddies who does have a contact in the area where I need help.

For your cop character, generating leads or getting the information needed can be as simple as picking up the phone.

- Is your LEO a Networker or does s/he rely on friends to get the information needed?

Q&A

What is the difference between a Police Officer, Sheriff's Deputy, Highway Patrol Officer and the State Police?

In the State of California there basically is no difference. All four are Peace Officers and are empowered by the California Penal Code with Police Powers anywhere in California.

A City Police Officer works for the specific city in which they are hired. For instance, the San Diego Police Department (SDPD) is an independent Police Agency operating specifically within the City of San Diego.

A Sheriff's Deputy works for the County Sheriff's Department. California is divided into counties. Where the individual communities have not incorporated into cities, the Sheriff's Department is the Law Enforcement Agency in charge. The Sherriff's Department also maintains County jails, Incarceration and Protection of Prisoners, Transportation of Prisoners to and from court, Security of Courts, and where requested provide contracted Law Enforcement Services. Most Cities prefer to maintain their own police department, however some cities (for various economical and political reasons) contract with the County for law enforcement. The contract usually provides for all the services of a normal police department.

The primary function of the California Highway Patrol (CHP) is the safe and efficient flow of traffic. Additionally the CHP enforces state statutes as they relate to traffic, assist allied agencies when called upon and during all large scale emergency incidents. When the California State Police merged with the CHP in 1995, the CHP picked up the added duties of ensuring the safety and security of state buildings and state property.

What are the different levels of crime?

Infraction, Misdemeanor, Felony, and Juvenile Crime.

Infractions – Crimes where the worst possible punishment is some type of monetary fine. Infractions are considered 'Arrests' because if the violator refuses to sign the citation/ticket, they have to be taken into custody (arrested) and taken before a Magistrate. If it is outside of court operating hours, the violator can spend the night in jail while waiting to see a Judge.

Misdemeanor – Driving Under the Influence (DUI), Petty Theft, etc are lesser crimes and the person arrested will be taken to a Police or Sheriff jail and booked. This potentially includes the person being fingerprinted and having their identity checked and verified. The Arrestee (in most cases) is released on a promise to appear citation. If the person is considered a flight risk they can be held in jail until the Court Date. DUI's are usually held at the jail until they are sober enough to adequately care for themselves.

Felony – Serious crime. Assault, armed robbery etc. Felony arrestees are usually held until their Arraignment, approximately two business days. Depending on the Felony, the Arrestee may be given the option of bailing out of jail. Murder suspects usually require a bail hearing in front of a Judge who decides whether the person is granted bail. If the Judge allows bail, he also sets the amount.

Juvenile Crime – Juveniles are treated differently than the above. First, when a Juvenile is taken into custody they can't, under any circumstances, be exposed to adult criminals. Depending on the jail facility, that could mean bringing the Juvenile in through a public entrance and holding them in an interview room. Once in custody, for the most part, the arresting officer has basically two choices: To book the Juvenile into a Juvenile holding facility (such as Juvenile Hall) or release them to their parent/guardian.

Citizen's Arrest – California Citizens have the right/authority to arrest another person for a criminal act. The act must be committed in the Citizen's presence. In essence, the citizen making the arrest must witness the transgression to have the authority to arrest for it. Depending on the law broken, a California Peace Officer may need to have the witnessing citizen place the wrongdoer under Citizen's Arrest.

When a private person makes a Citizen's Arrest, the responding officer may have the private party sign a private person's arrest form. Once the form is filled out, the Officer will take the arrested person into physical custody. At that point, the officer has the choice of either allowing the arrested person to sign a citation as a promise to appear in court or book them into jail. The person who makes a Citizen Arrest will more than likely have to testify in court.

How many years can a person who's bound for Detective-hood spend on patrol? Besides Narcotics, Robbery, Gang, what units are there for cities? I'm Canadian and know a little more about that side of things. Naming might be different, Mounties vs. city police and that sort of thing come into play and I want my WIP to be American-ish ;)

A person who's goal is to get into Investigations (although I do like the sound of Detective-Hood, it makes me think of Robin Hood. Yes, I know he was against the Sheriff, but he had a really, REALLY good reason :-)) will usually have to first be off probation before they are able to apply to/for Investigations. Time in patrol is important because this is where the officer hones his/her skills as well as begins to make a name and establish a reputation. Most departments require an officer to spend a minimum amount of time on patrol, usually one to two years, before they are eligible for promotion or other special assignments.

For most, the more time in the field usually equates to a more varied experience. So the theory is the greater the amount of time you do in patrol, the better chance you have of getting your first choice when you decide to promote out. That is not always the case. Each time an officer 'puts in' (applies) for a specialty position or promotion, there is usually a selection process where supposedly the best candidate is chosen. It's possible to have a two year rookie snatch up a position several five to seven year veterans requested, because that rookie has some hot new specialty skill or prior law enforcement experience with another agency.

Another thing to take into account is whether your officer has five years experience or one year experience five times.

An Agency's units are formed based on needs of the jurisdiction where they operate. Most jurisdictions have their own unique needs based on population, geographic location and tax base. For instance:

Is your Agency located near an International Airport?

Along a border?

Does it have a harbor?

Are there mountains?

What is the weather like?

Is it mostly urban?

Or mostly rural?

The above questions help a Police Agency determine which units would best serve the Community's needs and the Agency's vision.

The following chart is from the San Diego Police Department's (SDPD) website, as maintained by the City of San Diego: http://www.sandiego.gov/police/services/units/index.s html The chart is a very comprehensive list of all of SDPD's **Units** along with their **Responsibilities.** I thought it might be a help.

Note: Remember the units can change based on City and Community needs.

Air Support Unit
  • Provides air support to patrol operations in assigned areas.
  • Provides surveillance of persons engaged in criminal activities.

- Flies photographic missions for gathering of evidence, planning, critiquing, and surveying.
- Provides aerial security for V.I.P. and foreign dignitaries.
- Performs search and rescues involving downed aircraft and lost or stranded persons.

Armory – SWAT

- Performs hostage rescues and responds to special weapons and tactics emergencies.
- Serves high risk warrants and does dignitary protection.
- Provides fire control support.
- Removes barricaded individuals.
- Provides counter sniper capability.
- Provides chemical agent support and special events.

Auto Theft Unit

(http://www.sandiego.gov/police/services/units/autotheft.shtml)

- Reduction and prevention of vehicle thefts.
- Assists with the recovery of stolen vehicles and prosecution of those that steal vehicles.

Background Investigations

- Conducts personal History investigations on all applicants, i.e. recruits, reserves, etc.
- Insures POST employment inquiries for outside police agencies.
- Maintains background files on all applicants.

Canine Unit

- Conducts searches for suspects and lost persons.
- Conducts searches for evidence or contraband such as narcotics or explosives.
- Assist in felony warrant service.
- Supports Patrol, SWAT, Narcotics Task Force, Narcotics Section and other units.
- Utilizes dogs as an alternate use of force.

Child Abuse

- Conducts criminal investigations of child abuse, sexual molests, child neglect, and child exploitation.
- Develops Child Abuse Prevention Programs and cooperates with agencies providing preventative child abuse services.

Cold Case Homicide Unit
(http://www.sandiego.gov/police/services/units/coldcase/index.shtml)

- Investigates unsolved homicide cases.

Communications

- Answers primary emergency 911 calls originating within the City.

- Serves as primary phone answering point for requests for police service from the public.

- Dispatches officers when appropriate; refers or transfers calls to various departments or agencies.

Crime Analysis

- Provides information and resources to support Community Policing, Problem Solving and the Department's strategic planning efforts.

- Researches new developments and technology advancements to further Intelligence-Led Policing efforts.

- Develops tools and analysis to suppress crime, apprehend criminals and improve safety.

- Provides street level support to patrol officers to combat crime trends.

- Provides analytical support to investigators to assist with suspect identification and apprehension.

- Utilizes geographic information services (GIS) to support tactical and strategic efforts targeting criminals and reductions in crime.

Criminal Intelligence

- Collects intelligence information relating to organized crime and investigation of specific prosecution-oriented investigations.
- Coordinates with law enforcement officials of Mexico in the investigation of crimes.
- Contacts representatives of labor and management on a meet-and-confer basis.
- Maintains the computerized portion of the Informant System.

Crisis Intervention

- Provides immediate emotional and practical support to victims, witnesses, and other survivors involved in current traumatic situations.
- Provides 24 hr call-out via Communications.
- Notifies family, friends, and clergy and helps arrange follow-up services.

Data Systems

- Develops, installs and maintains the Department's computer systems and network.

Domestic Violence Unit

(http://www.sandiego.gov/police/services/units/domesticviolence.shtml)

- Assists with TRO's while officers are in the field.

- Handles all domestic related crimes.
- Responds to domestic violence cases as needed.

Elder and Dependent Abuse
(http://www.sandiego.gov/police/services/units/elderabuse/index.shtml)

- Identify individuals who prey on senior and dependent adult citizens
- Seek prosecution of these perpetrators.
- Develop good working relationships with the community and organizations

Equal Employment Opportunities (EEO)

- Investigates violations of equal employment policies and legislation.
- Educates Department Personnel on issues regarding job discriminations and E.E.O.
- Serves as a liaison for employers and employees.

Field Training Officer Administration (FTO)

- Coordinates probationary officer training for newly hired officers.
- Assigns trainees to FTO's.
- Counsels and disciplines trainees.
- Supervises field training officers.

Financial Crimes

(http://www.sandiego.gov/police/services/units/financialcrimes/index.shtml)

- Investigation of criminal offenses involving forgeries, check cases, credit card offenses, fraudulent credit applications, bunco-fraud schemes, embezzlements, computer crimes, bigamy cases and elder fiduciary abuse cases.

Forensic Science

(http://www.sandiego.gov/police/services/units/forensicscience/index.shtml)

- Analyzes physical evidence collected at crime scenes.

Gangs

(http://www.sandiego.gov/police/services/units/gangs.shtml)

- Identifies and investigates gang members and gang activity.
- Maintains the Department's gang information files, and maintains liaison with nationwide agencies with similar responsibilities.
- Assists patrol with gang information.

Harbor Patrol

- Patrols the waters of Mission Bay Park and the adjoining parklands.
- Investigates all boating accidents occurring on the Bay.

- Assists Lifeguard Harbor Patrol in providing rescue and first aid services.

Homicide

- Conducts criminal investigations of homicides.
- Conducts investigations of questionable suicides and deaths occurring under mysterious or unusual circumstances.
- Conducts investigations of officer involved shootings when an injury or death occurs.
- Provides information and assistance to agencies in other jurisdictions regarding homicide investigations.
- Investigates unsolved homicides (Homicide Evidence Assessment Team – HEAT)

Internal Affairs

- Investigates complaints of employee misconduct.
- Maintains files of complaints on sworn and non-sworn personnel.
- Investigates officer-involved shootings.
- Processes claims against the Department.

Juvenile Services

(http://www.sandiego.gov/police/services/units/juvenileservices/index.shtml)

- Coordinates the Intervention Program and monitors the Interagency Group.
- Supervises the Runaway Program and coordinates follow-ups with area Juvenile Sergeants and Intervention Officers.
- Maintains liaison with Probation, District Attorney (Juvenile), Juvenile Court, California Youth Authority, school administration, community based agencies, and others.
- Researches and develops delinquency prevention programs.
- Develops, coordinates, and trains officers and supervisors involved in juvenile programs.

Laboratory

- Conducts technical analysis of all forms of evidence.
- Conducts narcotics, polygraph, and alcohol analysis (drunk driver expert testimony).
- Does document and fingerprint examination (Cal ID Computer Program).
- Examines firearms for weapon ID, automatic weapons, silencers, drugfire computer I.D.

program, bullet matching, and gunshot residue.

- Uses forensic biology to analyze blood, semen, saliva, hair, and D.N.A.

- Examines trace evidence (hairs, fibers, arson, shoes/tires impressions, gunshot residues).

- Collects evidence and reconstructs crime scenes.

- Performs specialized photography (darkroom services).

- Develops latent prints with chemicals, powders, lasers, and photography.

- Impounds narcotics.

Legal Advisors

- Advises Administration on legal matters.

- Reviews policies and procedures for legality.

- Reviews discipline packages for conformance with Department policy and law.

- Represents Administration in personal matters.

- Reviews document requests and represents Department in court when necessary.

- Represents Department in other court proceedings and before the City Council.

Metro Arson Strike Team (MAST)

- Investigates suspicious fire and explosive incidents.
- Investigates post blast investigations.
- Investigate suspicious devices.

Media Relations

- Monitors news coverage.
- Trains the academy sergeants and others in media relations.
- Researches issues and writes speeches for the Chief.
- Deals with the media and citizen complaints.

Mounted Enforcement Unit

- Participates in crowd management
- Conducts canyon searches
- Conducts demonstrations and public speaking events.

Narcotics

- Focuses on illegal narcotic manufacturers, sale and possession, as well as organized crime, and narcotic dealers.

Neighborhood Policing

- Establishes and supports crime prevention programs.

- Provides training for trainers, officers, supervisors, managers, other agencies, and community members.

- Plans and facilitates monthly Problem Solving meetings.

- Provides resource development and networking to facilitate existing and proposed resources at all levels of city, county, state, and federal government and with private and public agencies.

Permits & Licensing (Vice Administration)
(http://www.sandiego.gov/police/services/units/permits.shtml)

- Administers all laws related to police-regulated businesses such as firearms dealers, card rooms, adult entertainment, secondhand dealers, pawn shops and massage establishments.

- Maintains the alarm permit system and investigates permit violations.

Personnel

- Maintains information on employment opportunities and personnel employment records

- Coordinates in-house selection interviews and hiring

- Issues badges and identifications cards

- Compiles Department personnel statistics and rosters.

Psychological Services

- Conducts pre-employment psychological screening.
- Provides confidential counseling and psychotherapy.
- Consults management; coordinates special services and workshops.
- Debriefs at SWAT Team call outs and other critical incidents.
- Conducts Peer Resource Support training.

Records

- Processes data, enters and maintains original files including arrest, crime, juvenile contacts, traffic accidents, citations, field interviews, and other related documents
- Conducts Cal-ID fingerprint searches
- Updates law enforcement systems on stolen vehicles, missing persons, and wanted property.

Recruitment

- Gives presentations on law enforcement careers to schools, colleges and community groups.

- Attends career days and job fairs and conducts recruit officer orientations.
- Conducts practical physical agility tests for applicants and does physical ability testing.
- Develops advertisement campaigns which target women and people with color.
- Establishes and maintains working relationship with Academy staff and the community.

Robbery

- Investigates commercial extortion's and kidnaps for reward.
- Investigates bank, commercial, residential, public transportation, and delivery persons or employees carrying or depositing commercial funds or property robberies.
- Assists area stations with series investigations.
- Provides surveillance and stakeout support for other units.

School Task Force

- Provides enforcement of laws on and around secondary schools.
- Serves as liaison with School Police and Administrators.

- Provides an ongoing truancy enforcement program.
- Works with City schools in drug prevention and gang enforcement programs.
- Conducts classroom presentations on a variety of police related subjects

Sex Crimes

http://www.sandiego.gov/police/services/units/sexcrimes/index.shtml

- Investigates felony sexual assaults involving victims fourteen years of age and older, including cases with juvenile suspects.
- Works with the District Attorney's Office and Victim Witness Assistance to assist victims in preparing for court appearances.
- Cross reports suspected cases of child abuse and works with the Department of Social Services when investigating cases which include protective issues.
- Acts as a liaison with physicians and nurse examiners at contract hospitals providing forensic examinations.
- Coordinates the Sexual Assault Speakers Bureau which gives presentations on the Sexual Assault Response Team and sexual assault prevention to community service groups, military personnel, high school, college and university students.

• Works with the Department of Justice to
register, track and monitor the 2800 sex
offenders living in the City of San Diego.

Special Investigations

• Identifies, surveils, and apprehends series
criminals.

• Identifies and recovers stolen property.

• Develops and maintains reliable sources of
information.

• Provides assistance to other units and other
law enforcement agencies.

SWAT/SRT (Special Response Team)

• Provides high risk warrant service,
dignitary/witness protection and special
tactics training programs for department
personnel.

• Provides fire control, chemical agent
support, and countersniper capability.

• Removes barricaded individual and
performs hostage rescue operations.

• Administers and oversees the Primary
Response Team program.

Traffic
http://www.sandiego.gov/police/services/units/traffic/index.shtml

• Serves the entire City and is comprised of the
Abandoned Vehicle Abatement Unit (AVA),

the Accident Investigation Bureau (AIB), Motors Unit, Parking Enforcement, and the Traffic Investigations Unit (TIU).

Vice Operations

- Enforces prostitution laws by conducting investigations and making arrests relating to the activities of prostitutes and pimps both on the street and operations under the guise of modeling, massage, and escort services.

- Conducts regular inspections and takes enforcement action at bars, liquor stores, and all other establishments licensed by Alcohol Beverage Control (ABC).

- Screens new liquor license applications to ABC and evaluates potential impact of such licenses on the community; conducts training for ABC-licensed businesses to help their employees recognize false ID's and detect other violations.

- Enforces gambling laws by investigating illegal horse race and sports betting, card and dice games, slot machines, and rigged gaming devices, bingo games and casino nights.

- Investigates organized cock fights, dog fights, and other violations of animal gaming laws.

- Conducts regular inspections of police-regulated businesses such as card rooms, cabarets, pool halls, peep booths, and nude entertainment establishments.

Would a man or woman be a 'person of interest' before they became a suspect? Do I have that reversed, or are there other terms?

A 'person of interest' is just that, someone Law Enforcement wants to talk to for clarification of 'things'. Usually, the term 'person of interest' is used when there is not quite enough information/evidence to label the person a suspect. Person of Interest could also be a witness or accomplice.

What is too young to be a New York Police Department Detective?

As far as the age of a Detective, it varies from agency to agency.

For New York Police Department (NYPD), a person can be selected in the academy to move to a specialty unit like Organized Crime Control Bureau (OCCB) or Narcotics, at any age. That person can have a certain 'look' (very young), skill set (speaks a certain language), knowledge or have connections. My cousin (NYPD – Patrol), and a friend (surprise, suprise – a NYPD Detective), tell me this doesn't happen all that often despite what the jaded rank and file believe.

However, further along the promotion chain can be a totally different story.

In the NYPD, being pulled into a specialty unit early doesn't automatically make the chosen officer a detective, their position is still that of a regular officer and it takes eighteen months before they are promoted to Detective 3 and receive their gold shield. Then it takes another eighteen months before being eligible to even be recommended for Detective 2. A supervisor or other command personnel has to recommend a Detective 3 for promotion, however getting Detective 2 is not automatic with a recommendation. I was told it took at least two to three recommendations before a person received their Detective 2.

Getting to Detective 1 is quite hard. A person can be at Detective 2 for ten years or more. Based on who you talk to, this level (Detective 1) is quite political. Some say this is where who you know or who you 'blow' (direct quote there) can get you grade faster.

Detective positions have both the undercover (U/C) and the investigator types. Most start off in a U/C capacity and as their investigation skills increase become the plain cloth Detectives people think of when Detective is mentioned.

A couple of things re: promotion to Detective. NYPD Detectives, within the department, have no more power or authority than a patrol cop. Detectives cannot order around a patrol officer. Yes, I know it happens a lot on TV, but that account is wrong. Detectives are simply considered an extension of a Patrol cop.

Here is where it can get a bit confusing (well for me at least;-P) Patrol Cops belong to the Patrol Benevolent Association (PBA) while Detectives belong to the Detective Endowment Association (DEA). Each Association dictates hours worked, pay scale and benefit package.

Detective 3 receives a pay raise of $7,000 annually over patrol officers. Detective 2 makes about the same as a Patrol Sergeant. Detective 1 is paid equal to a lieutenant. Detectives get eighteen less days off a year than patrol and may be required to work longer shifts.

So if a detective gets in trouble, he is simply moved somewhere else, like to a different Precinct, unless, of course, he is fired.

If a detective or patrol officer should decide they want to become a Sergeant, they test for it. Then, if they receive the promotion, they move to another union, the Sergeants Benevolent Association, where again their hours, etc., is changed. Once a detective makes sergeant, they can never go back to detective.

And there is no such thing as Detective Sergeant.

RECAP: Detective 3 from patrol eighteen months automatic, Detective 2 after another eighteen months with recommendation from supervisor. It can take two to three or more recommendations to get a Detective 2 grade. Detective 1 very difficult.

What is the deal between other law enforcement agencies and the FBI?

I have to start this answer by saying there are definite differences between City, County, State, and Federal law enforcement. I can talk candidly about every agency (especially my own) but you have to remember, it's only my opinion.

Trash talking other agencies is a favorite LEO past time. Every agency has some quirk that is a point of contention. For instance:

City Cops are considered to either have a narrow focus (within their city limits only) or they're poachers (targeting criminals outside their city).

Sheriff Deputies tend to be hard asses because they usually start their career working in the jail.

State workers are viewed as mired in bureaucracy, it's been said they won't take a dump unless the proper forms are filled out.

FBI Agents are thought of as college graduates with no life experience foolishly allowed to carry weapons.

DEA Agents are seen as brainless cowboys.

The fact some crimes overlap jurisdictions and agencies, in my opinion, is the source of a lot of the dissention between Law Enforcement Agencies. One trait all cops have is the need to be in control. So, imagine the fun when three different agencies get together to discuss who is going to take lead on the case. We're not talking Task Forces here.

Also think Internal Affairs (IA). Most cops don't like officers within their own department if they happen to be part of IA. FBI is in essence the IA for every Agency in the USA. Of course, having another Agency able to step in and take over an investigation doesn't endear them to many LEOs either.

What are the personality types for FBI agents? Specifically the Behavioral Analysis Unit (BAU)? I've always been told they are geeks. Why do most LEO's call them Feebies? Are there alpha males?

Agents working Behavioral Analysis, at least the ones I've met, seemed confident in whom they were. Direct, to the point and focused. I've never spent time outside the job with these types of Agents (well not FBI – BAU; I did spend some time with my Agency's 'Profilers').

I would definitely classify the BAU Agents I worked with as Alpha types. Don't get me wrong, they had a bit of Geek mixed in, but they displayed such a deep confidence that it overshadowed everything else. I was amazed at how, on entering a room full of veteran LEOs, within minutes they commanded not only their attention but you could see an underlying deference there.

Oh, I need to add, all of the BAUs I know are definitely A-type personalities with varying degrees of OCD sprinkled in.

I usually called them Feebies because it was easier to say than FBI. Cops tend to nickname EVERYTHING, plus Feebies sort of rolls off the tongue. :D

The cops I've spoke to who were not BAU, were gun enthusiasts. One guy carried three guns on him, are most cops nuts?

Most LEOs view their weapon as a tool. However, as I stated earlier, LEOs are nothing if not competitive. Sometimes it boils down to bragging rights for who can carry the most concealed weapons or who has the neatest and newest gadget. One office's Tackleberry is another office's Range Master.

The other side of competiveness is being prepared for all contingencies. It only takes one time of being short of rounds during a gun fight or having a weapon malfunction that couldn't be fixed in the field to convince most officers of the merit of having a back up weapon or four. **Just. In. Case**.

Most cops' mantra: It's better to have and not need something rather than need something and not have it.

I know a lot of LEO's have problems at home, do Special Agents have as many problems?

In my opinion, Federal Agents have a rougher life than their local counterparts. I'm not sure you are aware, with very little advance notice, Federal Agents can be relocated across the country or on the other side of world. Yes, administration tries to get volunteers first, but if they can't – Enjoy Columbia and be sure to write.

That's my way of saying I, personally, think Feds have a rougher go of it because their jobs can literally tear a family apart.

Glossary of Slang Terms & Acronyms

These are words or phrases I've run across throughout my career. They can be department specific or regional. You've probably already seen most of them used, in my book(s)

Everyone in Law Enforcement loves acronym. I think we do it just to annoy the general public. Here are some of the most common used acronyms and, where necessary, their meanings. Some have double meanings and most are very crude. Where applicable, the cop interpretation is included.

I must warn you some of the phrases are a bit crude. It is not my intention to offend anyone, just inform.

10-10: A ten code used by the CHP meaning end of shift. It also means someone died. You know end of shift permanently.

10-10 Blanket: Yellow plastic blanket CHP officers use to cover dead bodies at accident scenes.

187: Penal Code Statute in the State of California that denotes Murder.

20002/20001: California Vehicle Code sections 20002 and 20001 are the sections covering hit and run drivers, (those drivers who are involved in an accident and leave the scene without giving their information). 20002 applies to hit and run drivers causing property damage only. 20001 covers hit and runs causing great bodily injury.

When an officer, usually male, refers to a woman as a 20002 he is basically stating he either has had or wants to have a very brief sexual encounter. A 20001 in the past tense means the encounter with the woman went badly. In the present tense it means the officer is highly motivated.

5 Oh: Like the television series Hawaii Five O. Street slang meaning police.

5150: A California Welfare and Institutions Code police use to have a mentally unstable person reviewed for possible commitment. Usually means crazy person.

88: H is the eighth letter of the alphabet. 88 = HH = Heil Hitler, used by Neo Nazi's. You'd be surprised how many people have 88 tattooed on fingers, arms and written on paperwork.

Adam Henry: Or Circle with a dot in the middle. Adam Henry = A.H. or A** Hole.

Are you LE?: A way one cop asks another person if they are Law Enforcement.

ATF: Alcohol Tobacco, Firearms & Explosives. **Cops**: All Together, FIRE.

Back-up: Assisting an officer with a call or stop. It usually means *move you're a**,* things could get out of hand fast.

Badge Heavy: This type of person throws their weight around (pushes/intimidates people) based upon the authority given to them by their position (badge). Not a good thing.

BMW: British Motor Works. **Cops:** Big Mexican Woman.

BNE: Bureau of Narcotic Enforcement. **Cops**: Bullsh*t Never Ends.

Break-in (AKA Field Training): When a cadet graduates from a police academy they become a probationary officer, aka trainee. All trainees ride in a patrol car with a seasoned officer whose job it is to teach the new trainees how to put all of their academy knowledge and training to practical use. This is a very stressful and short period of time, between two and six months depending on the agency, when you are evaluated to see if you can adapt theory to practical application.

Break leather: Pull your gun.

Bogie: If one male officer on surveillance asks another male officer over the radio, *"Do you see that bogie at 9* *o'clock?"*, he is pointing out a female, usually scantily clad, that should not be missed. Other male officers out on surveillance will normally begin asking for a cross street.

Burned: Target of a surveillance recognizing he is under surveillance

Buy Money:Money that is used to purchase something, usually narcotics, during an undercover operation. The money is photocopied and the serial numbers recorded.

CA-DOJ: California Department of Justice

CHP: California Highway Patrol. **Cops**: Triple A (AAA) with a gun.

Check your six (6): A warning to watch your back/be careful.

CI: Confidential Informant

CRI: Confidential Reliable Informant

DEA: Drug Enforcement Administration. **Cops**: Don't Expect Anything, or Dumb, Educated A**holes.

DB: Depends on context. Usually means Dead Body or Detective Bureau.

Deuce: Drunk Driver. The original vehicle code violation for driving under the influence was 502 V.C. Cops shortened it to 2 or Deuce. Others claim the term comes from a person so intoxicated they are seeing double.

DOJ: U.S. Department of Justice

Door shaker: Security Guard.

Double Tap: Most police agencies train their officers to shoot twice in rapid fire sequence.

DRE: Drug Recognition Expert/Evaluator. A person trained to evaluate people possibly under the influence drugs. Based upon the evaluation they offer an evaluation and opinion as to that person's impairment.

DUI: Driving Under the Influence. Could be alcohol, illicit drugs or prescription drugs.

Failure Drill: Two shots to the body, one to the head. Done when an officer suspects a person is wearing body armor or hyped up on drugs.

Failure to yield: A vehicle that will not pull over for your red light. This usually turns out to be a person who's not paying attention, i.e. HUA, or a person under the influence of alcohol, drugs or stupid.

FBI: Federal Bureau of Investigation. **Cops**: Funny Business Incorporated, Fu*king Bunch of Idiots, or Famous But Incompetent.

Flying your patches: When a LEO drives their personal car with their uniform hanging in the window or otherwise visible to the public. Or, a LEO driving their personal car while wearing their uniform shirt and no cover shirt. This is usually done only by new officers or idiots! Once their car gets keyed or they are followed this behavior usually stops.

FPS: Fine piece of sh*t.

Fried: Target of a surveillance not only recognizing he is under surveillance, but has identified who was following him.

FUBAR: Fu*ked Up Beyond All Recognition. A situation that has gone in the toilet, usually because of one person.

FYI: For Your Information.

Golden Boy/Girl: A person in favor with management. Usually viewed as never being able to do anything wrong. Other officers may or may not like the golden person. Sometimes jealously gets in the way. Golden people get the best assignments.

Handoff: Giving or passing a case along to another team.

HBD: Had Been Drinking. Normally means the person is not drunk enough to go to jail.

HIDTA: High Impact Drug Trafficking Area

HMFIC: Head Mother Fu*ker In-Charge.

HUA: Head up A**

I'm on the job/Are you on the job?: A way a cop announces to another cop that they are in fact a cop. Or way to indirectly ask another if they are a cop.

I've got your back: A statement not made lightly or taken lightly. A statement of unwavering support. As with most things, cops consider the source of the statement.

LEO: Law Enforcement Officer

Lopp: A lazy police officer.

Meth Maggot: Chronic methamphetamine user. Usually has scabs and open sores.

Mexican Ounce: 25 grams.

Mr. 20%: A person who, on their best day, gives you a 20% effort.

One time: Street slang meaning police. From police officers habit of say "I'm only going to tell you this one time."

Narc: Undercover Narcotics Officer

OIC: Officer-in-Charge. An officer who is in the role of acting supervisor.

Oz: Ounce. 28.5 grams.

POS: Piece of sh*t.

Pursuit: A vehicle actually trying to evade and lose the police. This person is usually very reckless with their driving and their dismissal of all traffic laws. Very dangerous for both the public and the pursuing officers alike.

Q-tip: A very old person driving a car. From the back all you can usually see is their grey hair around the top of the driver's seat.

ROADy: Retired on Active Duty. A very lazy police officer.

SNAFU: Situation Normal All Fu*ked Up.

SO: A way of referring to a Deputy Sheriff or Sheriff Department

Stash Pad: Houses that are virtually empty except for a mattress to sleep on and large amounts narcotics stored throughout the house

TFO: Task Force Officers

T-stop: Traffic stop. Stopping a car for a traffic violation.

Tweeker: Chronic methamphetamine user who is so hyped up on the drug they are bouncing off the walls.

U/C: Undercover officer or agent.

Walk Over: Talking on the radio at the same time another is transmitting, the result is an incoherent garbled mess.

Wannabe: Slang (want to be). Refers to a security guard or other cop enthusiast who tried to become a cop but failed. This person can and usually does make a nuisance of themselves. Considered a derogatory remark. FYI: only nuisances are considered wannabes.

Warning shot: A miss. Some departments allow officers to fire a warning shot when use of deadly force is warranted. In reality an officer will tell you they fired a warning shot when they missed. The trick is explaining three to four warning shots.

About the Author

M.A. Taylor spent over twenty years in law enforcement. The first seven years were with the California Highway Patrol (CHP), although she loved the fun and excitement of patrol, her experiences during special assignments left her wanting more. Margaret left the CHP to become a Special Agent for the California Department of Justice (DOJ), spending over ten years in Narcotics. Four of those years Margaret was assigned to a Federal DEA-HIDTA Task Force. In the Division of Gambling Control (DGC), she investigated Tribal Casinos and California Card Clubs. Margaret moved over to California Bureau of Investigation (CBI) and specialized in sexual predators. Her areas of expertise range from surveillance to wiretaps to Tribal Gaming, sexual predators and many others.

See my website HTTP://www.MATaylor1010.com for upcoming workshops, on-line and in person.

Upcoming Books

Narcotics 101 Fall 2013
Sex Crimes 101 Winter 2013/14
Homicide 101 Spring 2014

How to contact Me

MA.Taylor@MATaylor1010.com

About *From a Cop's Viewpoint Investigations: 101*

Have you ever wondered about the differences between City, State and Federal Law Enforcement? How about, who's really in charge and why? What about the basic approach cops take when tackling a crime?

If you've had any of the above questions, From a Cop's Viewpoint: Investigations 101 is the place for you. Investigations 101 is written as a combination anecdotal, source and procedural book for writers wanting to accurately portray law enforcement, both in characterization and in investigational procedure. This book was written to hopefully entertain while imparting knowledge. My goal is to make the journey enjoyable for writers and non-writers alike.